DEADLY
DETOURS

Other books by Bob Briner

Lambs Among Wolves
Squeeze Play
Roaring Lambs

DEADLY DETOURS

Seven Noble Causes That Keep Christians from Changing the World

BOB BRINER

ZondervanPublishingHouse

Grand Rapids, Michigan

A Division of HarperCollinsPublishers

This book is dedicated to
Robert Archie Smith and Howard J. Krober,
coaches who did their best to keep me off the sidelines
and in the game—in the only game that really counts.

Deadly Detours
Copyright © 1996 by Robert A. Briner

Requests for information should be addressed to:

ZondervanPublishingHouse
Grand Rapids, Michigan 49530

Library of Congress Cataloging-in-Publication Data

Briner, Bob.
Deadly detours : seven noble causes that keep Christians from changing the world /
Bob Briner.
    p. cm.
    Includes bibliographical references.
    ISBN: 0–310–48630–0 (hardcover : alk. paper)
    1. Evangelicalism—United States. 2. Evangelistic work—United States. 3.
Christianity and politics—Controversial literature. 4. United States—Moral conditions.
5. United States—Church history—20th century. I. Title.
BR1642.U5B75 1996
277.3' 0829–dc20   95-49457
                                                     CIP

This edition printed on acid-free paper and meets the American National Standards
Institute Z39.48 standard.

Published in association with Sealy M. Yates, Literary Agent, Orange, CA 92668

Edited by Jan M. Ortiz
Interior design by Sue Koppenol

Printed in the United States of America

---

96 97 98 99 00 01 02 03/❖ DH/ 10 9 8 7 6 5 4 3 2 1

Contents

ACKNOWLEDGMENTS

Dr. Ray Pritchard, senior pastor at Calvary Memorial Church in Oak Park, Illinois, has been a wonderful source of help with Scripture questions. Any errors in this area are mine, not his.

I also acknowledge the help and insights provided by Dr. Sidney Chapman, who leads a regular Bible study in the home of our friends. His faithful ministry is recognized with appreciation and gratitude.

Bill Bullard began ministering to me thirty years ago, when I was a young college coach, and has never stopped. He will be mentioned in the text, but I want to thank him here and acknowledge my debt to him.

Finally, my wife, Marty, who knows more about the Scriptures than I ever will and who models that knowledge daily in our home, teaches me all the time by precept and example. I am thankful for her.

—RAB
Greenville College
Greenville, Illinois
November, 1995

ONE

WHO TOOK THE EVANGEL OUT OF EVANGELICALISM?

This is a tough book. It was tough to write and I am afraid that it will be tough to read. However, I pray that you will stay with me all the way, carefully examine what I have to say, ask God to guide you, and, most of all, test these concepts against Scripture. If you do this, it will help you avoid "deadly detours" and propel you down "heavenly highways" of joy and fulfillment as you obey scriptural commands and become more fully, vitally, and productively engaged in building God's kingdom.

With this book, I am personally departing from the numbers question that so dominates my professional life. I am not asking how many of these books will be sold. I may be writing this book for only one person. Maybe it is for me. Maybe it is for the one who types the manuscript. Maybe it is for my editor. Maybe no one will actually buy the book.

Maybe only one person will buy it. I leave this entirely in God's hands. Now, this does not mean that I want my publisher to do anything less than a first-class job of promoting, advertising, and distributing the book, or that I will not do the author's tours, book signings, and media interviews necessary to bring the book to the attention of potential readers. That would be poor stewardship. It does mean, however, that I am completely and totally relaxed, and if no one reads the book, that will be okay. I have obeyed and done what I believe God told me to do.

There are other books that I wanted to write far more than I wanted to write this one. There are other books I was scheduled to write before writing this one. However, God had other plans. I believe he has directed me to write this book at this time.

Now, think of all the people you know. Think of all the Christians you know. I must tell you that I am probably less mystical than any of your acquaintances. You need to know that I live my life and make my living out in the rough-and-tumble world of big-time professional sports and television. This is the world of the ultimate pragmatist. Only the bottom line counts. The most common question in my business is, What are the numbers? Particularly with the professional golfers but with all sports and in television, the questions are, How many people came? How many bought tickets? How many tuned in to the telecast? What were the ratings? How many advertisers bought "spots"? How much did they pay? What were the production costs and the rights fees? How much did we clear? What was the bottom line? What are the numbers? It always boils down to the numbers.

I tell you all this so that you will know how unusual it is for someone with my lifestyle, how unusual it is for *me,* to say, "God told me to do this"—something that I have never said before. Certainly more and more I believe in his leading. I believe that the Holy Spirit guides us daily, and I firmly believe in a Scripture-directed life. Even believing all this, however, is a far cry from saying, "God told me to do this—this very specific thing—to write this book at this time." This probably tells you more about my inner life, my spiritual depth, or lack thereof, than is wise when I am trying to draw you into this book and am asking you to believe and act on what it says. But, because this is such a tough book, I feel the need to be as open, honest, and up-front with my readers as I know how to be—especially if there is to be any chance that this book will accomplish what I believe God wants it to accomplish.

A major part of the promotion of my first book, *Roaring Lambs,* involved radio. I was the guest on dozens of both secular and Christian radio programs all around the country, many of which were call-in programs. The typical format would involve the host's interviewing me, often in some depth, about the content and message of the book, followed by questions and comments phoned in by listeners. The point I tried very hard to make in *Roaring Lambs* is that we need to take the scriptural command to be "salt" very seriously and that each of us can obey the command by being alert to opportunities to tell in a positive way who Jesus is and why he came. I tried to show that every Christian has both the responsibility and the opportunity to do this on a regular basis, regardless of age, abilities, geography, or gender. To tell who Jesus is and why he came is the point of that book.

In most cases, the hosts of the radio programs had read and understood the book before we went on the air and used the interview time very adroitly to help me make the major point of the book. So far, so good. But almost invariably, *particularly on Christian stations*, the callers wanted to talk to me about almost everything except Jesus. They wanted to talk about how terrible television is, how awful the movies are, about prayer in public schools, about the homosexual agenda, about abortion, about pornography and child abuse, about sex education, and about politics. The disturbing thing is that most of the callers thought they were talking about Jesus! A typical conversation would go something like this:

Host: "You're on the air with Bob Briner. Do you have a question or comment about his book, *Roaring Lambs?*"

Caller: "I certainly do. Bob, I think your book is great. We need to do more to let the administration and the Congress know that we are sick and tired of such ungodly things as condom distribution in our schools."

Another very typical caller would say, "You sound like you may be a little soft on distributing condoms in school and the separation of church and state. Where do you stand on this?" Now, I had not said anything about either condoms or the Establishment Clause of the Constitution. I had been talking about who Jesus is and why he came. After this kind of thing happened over and over again, it began to make an impression—a disturbing one. Where was Jesus in the lives of the people?

If you read *Roaring Lambs,* you will already know that Sealy Yates is my literary agent, mentor, and friend. You will know that he is an outstanding Christian lawyer as well as *the* top Christian literary agent. In the recent past, Sealy has honored me by allowing me to participate in decisions that he is wrestling with related to his future career and ministry direction. With Sealy, these are not separate decisions. His family life, career, and ministry are all part of a seamless whole. He has integrated his life around his service to the person of Jesus Christ and the building of his kingdom.

Sealy's "problem" is one we would all like to have—too many abilities, too many talents, too many opportunities for service, too many people wanting a so-called piece of him. His successful law practice was taking too much time away from his successful literary agency—and vice versa. He recently decided that he really needed to make a choice. He needed to be either a full-time attorney or a full-time Christian literary agent. Thus, he asked friends to pray and counsel with him about his choice.

Sealy is a fine Christian attorney, but there are many fine attorneys—even several Christian ones. As a Christian literary agent, however, he is unique. He is in a position to bring Christian writers together with the right publishers to produce the optimum results for edifying the saints and building the kingdom of God. Writers trust him. Publishers trust him. He is special. Jesus matters in Sealy's life.

Often when wrestling with someone else's problem, we gain more than we give. Such was the case with Sealy and me. In thinking about his uniqueness as a Christian literary agent, I began to think more and more about the uniqueness of all Christians and what we are called to do, which is the first reason that I am writing this book. I write to make Jesus known.

A second reason that I am writing this book is found in music. I am a fan of southern-gospel music. I grew up and lived most of my life in Texas, so this kind of music is a part of my heritage. I love it. The simple messages, melodies, and rhythms are just right for this old Texan. Do not misunderstand me. I enjoy and appreciate a wide variety of musicians and musical styles, but, for me, a gospel quartet is something special. My favorite is the Cathedrals—guys who have been around and have stood the test of time. I have most of their cassettes, and they take their turn in my car tape deck along with Chuck Swindoll's teaching me Scripture, Steve Green's singing hymns, and the Gaithers performing their own wonderful songs. I have many favorites among the Cathedrals' repertoire, but lately one song, not particularly a favorite, has been almost constantly in my mind—"Jesus Is Right for Whatever's Wrong in Your Life"—a message that compels me to write this book.

A third reason that I am writing this book is found in the life of a very special mentor, Bill Bullard, whom I mentioned in my acknowledgments. Through God's grace I met Bill thirty years ago, and he has been ministering to me and teaching me ever since. Although I live in Texas and he lives in Michigan, we connect, we tune in, we communicate, we are in touch.

I first met Bill in Washington, where he played a major part in organizing the ongoing presidential prayer breakfast, the House and Senate prayer breakfasts, and prayer and Bible-study groups throughout our nation's capital. About the time I moved to Michigan to coach at Spring Arbor College, Bill moved to Michigan to organize the prayer-breakfast movement in that state. The Michigan governor's prayer breakfast, mayors' prayer breakfasts throughout the state, and many men's regular weekly prayer and Bible-study groups are the result of his efforts, his charisma, his organizational ability, and God's blessing on his life.

As far as I know, Bill Bullard is one of a kind—a complete ministerial free agent. He has no staff, no organizational structure, and is responsible only to the men to whom he ministers and to the God he serves so faithfully and so well.

There was a time when Bill would spend his time in organizing local core groups, city-wide, and even state-wide ministry efforts. There was a time when, if asked by others in ministry to help, even to go with them to foreign countries, he went to lend his special kind of organizational skill. No more.

Now he goes only to talk about Jesus. Whether he goes to Battle Creek or Beijing, it is to talk about Jesus. He does not go to organize anything; he goes only to talk about Jesus. Recently, some of his friends in the ministry wanted him to go with them to India to help Christians in leadership positions there organize various ongoing ministries. Bill told them, "Guys, I am just not into that anymore. If you want me to go and talk about Jesus, I'll go, but not to organize anything."

In all my recent personal and telephone visits with Bill, this new interest in, and new love for, the person of Jesus has been obvious. He even thinks a new version of the New Testament is needed in which all the pronouns that refer to Jesus would be replaced by the name *Jesus*, focusing additional attention on the Savior.

Now, do not get the idea that Bill Bullard is some sort of ascetic, a deeply and mystically spiritual guy living some sort of rarefied existence. He and his wife live in Ann Arbor and have raised their children in this dynamic city dominated by the University of Michigan. Bill, a handsome guy who is always nattily dressed, moves easily with top business and governmental leaders in his state—the men to whom he ministers. He loves sports, business, politics, movies, and his family. He also loves Jesus and focuses on him more and more. Bill has always had a significant positive influence on me, but never more than now as he emphasizes one thing—really one person—Jesus. Bill's new emphasis is compelling.

I am continually reminded of how important Jesus is. My work often takes me away from home, and all too often I am forced to be away on Sunday. On these occasions, when it is not possible or practical to attend a worship service, I try to find something of spiritual substance on television in my hotel room. Sometimes I am able to find Charles Stanley, whom I know will give me solid biblical teaching. Often Robert Schuller's *Hour of Power* gives me an hour of inspiration and directs my thoughts toward worship.

On a recent Sunday, God led me to, I think for a particular reason, Jerry Falwell's *Old Time Gospel Hour*. The only problem was that there was no gospel in the hour.

This particular Sunday was shortly after the gay march on Washington, and the Rev. Jerry Falwell used almost the entire hour to sell videotapes that he said consisted of secret footage of gay activities involving and surrounding the march. Over and over, throughout the hour, viewers were "treated" to clips of some of the most bizarre and obnoxious of those poor benighted people who are advocating the terribly misnamed gay lifestyle. The Rev. Mr. Falwell told his viewing audience that we all needed to send $39.95 to get those tapes in order to learn about the gay agenda in America—as if it was a secret. To give viewers an added incentive to buy the tapes, Mr. Falwell promised to send along an additional tape of him making a bungee jump! Throughout the hour, clips of the gay march on Washington were interspersed with clips of the Rev. Mr. Falwell making his bungee jump, followed by a hard sell. This was *The Old Time Gospel Hour.* The only thing close to being accurate in the title was the fact it was an hour. It was not old time and there was no gospel. There was nothing about Jesus.

Dr. John Seel, of the Trinity Forum, the Christian think tank in Washington, recently sent me an audio cassette of presentations he and Dr. Os Guiness made at a Forum event in 1993. Both addresses had significant impact on me and dovetailed with the other experiences, both positive and negative, recounted above.

Os talked in a very solemn, sober way about the state of evangelical Christianity in America today. Where once the term *evangelical* had positive uplifting connotations, now it is a term almost of derision, associated with scandal at worst and superficiality at best. He said that evangelicalism was once characterized by a search for truth and an "I believe" way of identifying itself, but now it has lost much of its meaning and identity as it has drifted into being basically a movement associated with a series of causes—many of them political. As its longtime leaders—Billy Graham, Carl F. H. Henry, and Harold Lindsell—age and inevitably pass from the scene, there seem to be no comparable leaders ready to take their places. Os says that the movement is adrift, rudderless and directionless. Even the term *evangelicalism* has lost much of its currency and is often replaced in daily discourse by the horrible title, "the

Religious Right." What happened? According to Os Guiness, we abandoned "the first things of the Gospel." I must admit that I had not heard this phrase before, but in his presentation, Os used it over and over and over. "The first things of the Gospel," he said repeatedly, as forcefully and as powerfully as he could. "We must return to the first things of the Gospel."

During the days following my hearing Os's message, I asked many people what they thought Os meant by "the first things of the Gospel." I could not get the phrase out of my mind. It competed with the Cathedrals' song "Jesus Is Right for Whatever's Wrong in Your Life." My conversations with other Christians pretty much confirmed what I had concluded. The first things of the Gospel, I believe, are (1) that Jesus came and (2) that his kingdom is not of this world. When we forget either of these, when we fail to build our lives and our ministries around them, we cease to be truly evangelical, and we inevitably take deadly detours and miss heavenly highways.

Of the two first things of the Gospel, perhaps the hardest for us to remember is not that Jesus came but that his kingdom is not of this world. The people who called to talk with me on all the radio programs typically remembered that Jesus came but failed to remember that his kingdom is not of this world. They were so caught up in the cares, causes, concerns, and issues of the here and now that the real reason Jesus came, to establish a kingdom not of this world, escaped them.

It is extremely difficult to keep the things of time and space from completely overwhelming, from completely crowding out the things of eternity. John Seel says that because of modernity—the things that make up the way we live as we near the end of the twentieth century—it has never been harder for Christians to maintain a proper view of eternity, a proper view of the kingdom that Jesus came to establish. From computers to faxes, to space shuttles, to atomic medicine, to satellite communications, to technology of all kinds, the modern world controls modern man and dominates his thinking to such an extent that only God's constant help gives us any chance of seeing the paramount importance of the eternal kingdom of Jesus. However, in spite of the difficulty, in spite of modernity and all its problems, Christians must do everything possible to face life here in light of eternity. Unless we do, we are destined for deadly detours. Unless we do, we will miss the heavenly highway.

In my own life, a renewed emphasis on studying the Gospels has been a significant help. There is certainly nothing wrong with giving plenty of time to the Pauline epistles and all the other wonderfully vital and instructive New Testament writings, but we neglect the Gospels at our spiritual peril. We know the story so well that we tend to be neglectful of Matthew, Mark, Luke, and John. In doing this, we are apt to forget the first things of the Gospel. Most of all, we are apt to forget that it was Jesus, God's only Son, full of grace and truth, our wonderful, beautiful Savior who came. We need to think often on his life, his words, his actions, his death, and his resurrection—everything about him. We need to be reminded over and over, as often as possible, about his constant emphasis on the kingdom of God and the fact that it is not of this world.

As we read and study the Gospels, we need to be struck anew by Jesus' repeated descriptions of the fate of those who miss his kingdom. He tells us that it is much better to lose parts of our bodies than to be cast into hell, that on the day of judgment it "will be more bearable for Sodom and Gomorrah" than for those who miss his kingdom; that those who miss the kingdom will be thrown into "the fiery furnace where there will be weeping and gnashing of teeth"; that the fire will be eternal; that there will be darkness; that "their worm does not die, and the fire is not quenched"; that there will be torment and agony. These are Jesus' words.

These are tough teachings, not very fashionable in our day. Because of this and because we all too often do not see things from an eternal perspective, we can become very distraught about a single earthly death and yet can contemplate with equanimity multitudes being assigned to eternal torment in the fires of hell. We have it exactly backward. Jesus told us not to be afraid of those who kill the body, but to be afraid of those who can destroy both the soul and body in hell.

So, the point of this book is that we must think more and more about who Jesus is and why he came, remembering that his kingdom is not of this world and that the fire, darkness, weeping, agony, and torment of hell are real and that they are forever. If we really internalize this, it *will* change the way we approach our lives as Christians. It will change the way we use our spiritual gifts. It will change our approach to ministry. It will change our priorities. It will change the way we live our lives. It will keep us from taking deadly detours. It will bring us the joy that comes only with the knowledge that we are productively participating with Jesus in building his kingdom.

Having a kingdom view of life, seeing things from an eternal perspective, will in no way cause us to withdraw from the significant issues of this life. Never! On the contrary, it will cause us to be more deeply and more intimately involved. It will cause us to penetrate every human activity with the salt of the Gospel by changing our timing, strategies, approaches, procedures, and goals. We will never use methods to save lives on earth that will drive people away from the Savior, since this would obviously be not only counterproductive but also unthinkable (see particularly chapter 6 on abortion).

So, we must consider the question of how we should live. How should we live, if we want to be more successful in seeing the world as Jesus saw it? How should we live if we want to take the ultimate long view, the eternal view? In this book, I want to consider how we can avoid deadly, time-consuming detours, which we can do

- if we focus on the person of Jesus Christ;
- if we see him and the reason that he came as the motivation for all we do;
- if we believe and act on the belief that Jesus is right for whatever is wrong in our lives;
- if we understand that because we are Christians, we are peculiarly and uniquely qualified and specifically commanded;
- if we continually seek God's help in seeing all that we do, and all that we need to do, in light of eternity.

Then we will find that narrow way and walk it with joy.

Keeping the first things of the Gospel firmly in mind, let us do it together.

TWO

DEADLY DETOUR #1:
SQUABBLING OVER PRAYER
IN PUBLIC SCHOOLS

Satan must be enjoying a hearty laugh. The angels in heaven must be weeping. With so much that is vital to do, with the clock of history moving so rapidly forward, with so many souls dying without ever having heard a compelling presentation of who Jesus is and why he came, for so many Christians to spend so much time, energy, effort, and resources on the nonissue of legalizing school prayer is appalling and heartbreaking. The fight to legalize school prayer is a deadly detour.

Why do we get so caught up in, involved with, and exercised about such a frivolous public issue as whether or not pharisaic prayers can be offered in public schools? It is probably because it offers such an easy way to *feel* righteous. As

↑ rather than be righteous plus don't have to touch

fallen people, we look for the easy way, for cheap grace, which, it turns out, is almost always a deadly detour. As we blithely skip down the prayer-in-public-school road, millions die without knowing Jesus because we are not willing to do the hard work that God has called us to do.

It is easy to make a contribution to a church leader who says that he is fighting for prayer in public schools. It is easy to sign a petition to a congressperson or senator advocating that public-school prayer be made legal. It is easy to work up a case of righteous indignation when a school district prohibits a public prayer at graduation or a football game. It is easy to feel victorious when a basically inconsequential court decision allows for that shallow public prayer. But are we really involved, really engaged, in building God's kingdom?

In my own small church, a dear, dear brother in Christ, a man who has spent his whole life in service to his Lord, was moved to public proclamations of victory and joy when the Supreme Court recently ruled 9–1 that student-initiated public prayer at school functions was legal. Our wonderful pastor, a man whom I admire, led our congregation in a spontaneous prayer of thanksgiving to celebrate this so-called advance of God's kingdom. I had never seen our congregation more demonstrative.

Once it took true reformation, real revival fire, life-changing, culturel-shaping movements of the Holy Spirit to evoke outpourings of joy in the church. Now, we can work up feelings of blessing because a student can pray publicly at a graduation ceremony! Sad. I almost wept over this deadly detour.

The problem with waiting for our blessings to come from genuine revival is that revival takes prayer—prayers of commitment, prayers of brokenness and anguish, real prayer, secret in-the-closet prayer, continual prayer, fervent prayer, corporate prayers, and prayers where believers covenant together and are obediently asking the Father to send forth reapers. These kinds of prayer are already legal. No one is prohibiting them. There is no need to send $25 to Pat Robertson so his lawyers can battle in the courts on our behalf. There is no need to sign petitions to be able to pray these kinds of prayers. We need only petition the Father to help us for Jesus' sake. The problem is that it is hard to pray in these ways. It is so much easier to send a check, sign a petition, and feel good about ourselves. A deadly detour.

Do I wish that every class in every school was opened every day with a public prayer? Of course I do. Is it a big deal? No it is not!

Is it not just a little incongruous that we would make such a big deal over exactly the kind of prayer that Jesus denigrated? Public, oratorical, ceremonial prayer was not a big deal to him. Why is it such a big deal to us? Because it is easier to protest about prayer prohibitions in public schools than it is to do the real work of prayer, which no one can prohibit.

In fact, prayer is not really prohibited in public school. Thousands of Christian teachers and hundreds of thousands of Christian students (perhaps millions at exam time!) pray every day in public schools. The fact that their prayers are not audible and public probably adds to the prayers' effectiveness.

Why have we made the place of prayer such a big issue? Is praying for our schools more effective if done on school property than elsewhere? Is God limited in his ability to answer prayer because of the site from which the prayer emanates? Of course not. There is absolutely nothing that prohibits American Christians from bathing our principals, teachers, and students in prayer every day, except the will to do so. Certainly our schools and all those involved with them need prayer as never before. Let us stop playing games with this nonissue of legalizing prayer in school and really begin praying regularly and earnestly for our schools. This is the way to get off a deadly detour, to become focused. These days we hear much florid political and pulpit oratory decrying the fact that American school children no longer have the benefit of seeing and hearing their teachers pray for them. We seem to have a Norman Rockwellian vision of a godly teacher, standing in front of a class with uplifted eyes, praying, while the students bow reverently. I am afraid that even in the best of times that sort of occurrence was much more myth than reality. I was both a student and a teacher in days when classroom prayer was accepted, but I do not remember any revivals breaking out in any schools where I attended or taught. This is not to say that there have not been godly teachers who have modeled Jesus for their students. There were and still are. However, their effectiveness in being salt had, and has, little or nothing to do with oratorical prayer in their classrooms.

It has never really bothered me that my own children never saw or heard their teachers praying for them or heard a prayer broadcast over the public-address system to open their school day. If they got up early enough, they could see their own mother on her knees praying for them every day. They knew that their mother, father, grandmother, grandfather, and other family members prayed constantly for them. If we make prayer important in our homes, if our children know we believe in and are committed to prayer, and they see the effects of prayer in the lives of their own family, public prayer in schools becomes the nonissue it should be.

If Christians would stop and think, we would realize that legalized school prayer would present far more problems than it would solve. Those who fight so valiantly, so loudly, and at such great expense to legalize prayer in schools seem to think that there is a righteous Christian teacher in every classroom just waiting to be able to begin an effective fervent prayer ministry with his or her class. Such is far from the case. How would Christian parents react if their elementary child came home and said, "Mommy, today we said a prayer to the Great Spirit that lives in the trees and flowers and we learned that we are God ourselves. Isn't that neat?" Or, "Today we prayed to the same god that the boys and girls in India pray to. Tomorrow we get to pray to a different god, the one Japanese boys and girls pray to." This kind of thing is the inevitable outgrowth of legalized school prayer in a pluralistic society. Why do we want to spend our time, money, and effort fighting for this? It is a deadly detour.

The real issue behind school prayer is the spiritual condition of our children and their schools. Thankfully, as we avoid the deadly detour, there are many more positive things that we can do to influence the moral and spiritual conditions of our schools. There are many wonderfully meaningful things that we can do that are consistent with a belief that Jesus is right for whatever is wrong in your life and that contemplate his kingdom.

The first, as alluded to already, involves our own homes. Particularly if we have children or grandchildren in school, we need to be sure that we are praying regularly and specifically for their situations at school. We need to learn the names of their teachers and pray for them by name. We need also to pray for our local boards of education. Our children should see us in prayer and they should be told that their day at school is being committed to the Lord in prayer. A brief "Mom's prayer" where the mother places her hand on her children just as they rush out the door will be very meaningful. Our first priority should be to cover our children and their school fully in prayer that emanates from home.

Second, in our churches, those of us who are concerned about our children and our schools should see that there is regular ongoing, organized, scheduled prayer for the school-age children of the congregation, specifically as it relates to their school situation. Why do we schedule regular time to pray for our missionaries and leave our own children uncovered? That is backward. We need to pray for our children first and then the missionaries.

Finally, in addition to seeing that our homes and churches are fully involved in "school" prayer, we need to involve ourselves in specific school-related ministries. God has raised up some very effective ministries that focus particularly on public schools, for which we can be most thankful. Among the most impressive of these is Moms In Touch, International.

Moms In Touch exists for one reason: to promote effective prayer for children and their schools. The commitment, dedication, and singleness of purpose of the members are inspiring. They refuse to get sidetracked. Their constitution and bylaws are very precise and very specific. The intensity with which they guard against deadly detours is a challenge to us all. Consider some of their organizational imperatives, quoted from Moms In Touch, International—Policies and Guidelines:

1. MIT is not a lobbying group, regardless of how worthy the cause.

2. *Remember,* MIT prays for *our* children and all that pertains to their schools. Therefore, other topics for prayer need to be done before or after the MIT hour (emphasis MIT).

3. MIT strongly recommends that you do *not* have your prayer time on your school campus. We do *not* need to be seen. We do not want to do anything that will question the true, sincere motives of MIT (emphasis mine).

4. MIT does not sponsor videos, tapes, speakers, Christian programs, etc. *Remember, MIT is prayer.* If the Lord directs a mom to be a part of something wonderful in the school or community, great! But the name MIT may not be associated (emphasis mine).

5. MIT does not do any fund-raising. Because this statement is so unusual, it needs to be repeated with added emphasis. *MIT does not do any fund-raising.*

Do you think that those in Moms In Touch worry very much about what Congress or the Supreme Court says about prayer in schools? Of course not. They are too busy praying! They do not have time for deadly detours.

Another impressive aspect of the Moms In Touch program is that part of each of their prayer hours is set aside to pray scripturally. In each of these sessions, they pray a "scriptural passage together pertaining to praise, confession, thanksgiving, and intercession." Here are examples taken from actual Moms In Touch weekly prayer agendas:

Praise. "I love the LORD, for he heard my voice; he heard my cry for mercy. Because he turned his ear to me, I will call on him as long as I live" (Psalm 116:1–2).

Confession: "If we confess our sins, he is faithful and just and will forgive us our sins and purify us from all unrighteousness" (1 John 1:9).

Thanksgiving: "It is good to praise the LORD and make music to your name, O Most High, to proclaim your love in the morning and your faithfulness at night" (Psalm 92:1–2).

Intercession: "See to it that no one takes (insert your child's name) captive through hollow and deceptive philosophy, which depends on human tradition and the basic principles of this world rather than on Christ" (Colossians 2:8).

In their regular prayer time together, Moms In Touch pray conversationally (no oratorical, pharisaic prayers for them!) and practice what they call "one accord praying." Here, from their literature, is a description of it:

> ONE ACCORD PRAYING IS: *Spirit directed prayer.*
> The Holy Spirit within us moves on our hearts and initiates our requests as well as how we should pray. Therefore the focus is on God and not the approval of others.
> ONE ACCORD PRAYING IS: *Praying one subject at a time.* If a mom starts to pray on a particular subject, the other moms need to be keenly aware of her request. Hear her heart. Then when she is finished, other moms may feel free to pray on that subject as well. One mom could pray more than once on that subject if the Holy Spirit should so lead her. After that subject is exhausted

the Holy Spirit will lead another mom to pray a new subject.

ONE ACCORD PRAYING IS: *Making sure your prayer is brief, honest and to the point.* Your prayer should only be a few sentences. Remember, good conversation is letting someone else have a chance. It is not necessary to pray around the circle.

ONE ACCORD PRAYING IS: *Speaking in conversational language.* Speak to the Lord with the simplicity of a child talking to her Father. The more natural the prayer, the more real He becomes.

(Moms In Touch acknowledges the contributions that Rosalind Rinker's book, *Prayer, Conversing With God* [Grand Rapids: Zondervan, 1959] makes to the above.)

Moms In Touch provides access to a heavenly highway. If you think you should learn more about their efforts write to Moms in Touch, P.O. Box 1120, Poway, CA 92074-1120.

Whether Moms In Touch is the right organization for you or not (you may not be a mom with a child in school), I hope you will agree that it provides a way around a deadly detour for those who have a real kingdom concern about schools and the children who attend them. If school prayer is important, and, of course it is, a most effective way to pursue it is through Moms in Touch.

Just as Moms In Touch is an organization primarily involved with a ministry focused on elementary schools, Young Life is a ministry primarily focused on secondary schools, and it provides another way around a deadly detour for those who are not only committed to the first things of the Gospel but who also view eternity seriously. Put simply, my wife and I have found that Young Life is the finest, most productive ministry in which to be involved. This is in no way meant to denigrate Campus Crusade for Christ, the Fellowship of Christian Athletes, the Navigators, or InterVarsity. These organizations also have wonderfully effective Christ-centered campus ministries. I have just had more firsthand involvement with Young Life. It is a great organization, a great ministry.

While the politicians and the pulpit pounders are wringing their hands and trying to extract votes and/or dollars from you and me, Young Life is quietly working every day on high school campuses across America to present the person of Jesus Christ and his claims on the lives of teenagers. This group is tremendously effective.

A typical Young Life staff person is a college graduate, who is deeply committed to Christ and who has been thoroughly trained in how to build Christlike quality relationships with high school students. He or she becomes an integral part of the life of a particular school, asking nothing of the students except the chance to be a friend. Relationships develop and lead to opportunities to present Jesus.

While one-on-one relationships are at the heart of the Young Life ministry, two important group activities also take place each week when school is in session—Club and Campaigners. Club is a time for fun, after which there is a brief message from Scripture. Campaigners is a time for discipling kids through in-depth Bible study. Young Life also sponsors winter and summer camps. Many teenagers' lives have been changed forever as they meet Jesus through these great camping programs.

Young Life does require financial support because their "missionaries" are paid. If you have a real burden for high school students, maybe you should be on your local Young Life board.

Young Life has not forgotten the first things of the Gospel. They are on the front lines every day presenting Jesus Christ to America's teenagers on their own turf and in language they can understand. They have not taken the deadly detour. They need and merit your support and involvement. Pray for Young Life. There is no law against it. If you want to know more, write to Young Life, P.O. Box 520, Colorado Springs, CO 80901-0520.

American Christians have much more important things to do with our time, energy, and money than expend them in frivolous pursuits. We really must begin to take a look at our priorities. We need to measure everything we do against what we are uniquely and specifically called to do as followers of Christ. When we consider the first things of the Gospel, who Jesus is and why he came, when we remember what he tells us about his kingdom and about eternity, we will get a clear picture of what is really important. I do not think that we will see the fight to legalize school prayer in that picture. It is a deadly detour taking us away from the real ministry of prayer and witness, which is wide open to all who will hear the real call to serve our nation's schools and children. What we ought to do is: (1) pray regularly for our public schools, and (2) consider supporting the efforts of organizations such as MIT and Young Life who exist solely to nurture our schools effectively and legally.

There is a heavenly highway cutting across every school campus in America. Many are finding it. Millions more need to do so.

THREE

DEADLY DETOUR #2:
MAKING JESUS
A RIGHT WINGER

He is the only cause I'll own
Him I will make known
No politics of left or right
I only trust in God's true might
this world is not my home.

Bob Briner, *"The Only Cause"*

Of all the alluring deadly detours beckoning Christians in the 1990s, the most seductive is, without a doubt, politics. This should not come as a surprise when we stop to think about it. It was the detour that Jesus had to constantly warn his disciples against, even while he was with them. They asked him more than once about worldly power and prominence.

31

He told them more than once that his kingdom was not of this world. He continues to try to tell us the same thing. He calls us to concentrate on him, on his very specific instructions to us, on eternity, on a kingdom not of this world. We, though, seem not to listen and not to learn from the powerful lessons recorded in the Gospels.

It is easy to see how Jesus' disciples could be consumed by politics. They had been subjugated by a foreign power. The proud Jewish nation was under the heel of Roman conquerors. They longed for release from their oppressor.

It is also easy to see why American Christians heed the siren song of political action. For many, it seems that the reins of our government are held by those whose motives and goals are as foreign to us as those of the Romans were to the Jews. We are appalled by a government and a president who supports abortion, homosexuals in the military, and the funding of pornographic and blasphemous art. We are repelled by what we have heard about our president's moral character. But we must remember that as bad as we think things are for us here and now, they were infinitely worse for the Jews under the Romans. Yet Jesus continued to preach about, teach about, and emphasize a kingdom not of this world. He continued to exhort his followers to remain focused and not be distracted from the infinitely more important task of presenting him high and lifted up and of going into all the world and making disciples.

Many of the most visible Christian leaders, particularly those regularly on television, have contributed mightily to distracting American Christians from what Jesus really calls us to do, and disastrously so. Once the so-called television evangelists discovered that their contributions skyrocketed when they used their air time to bewail the evils of government and those directing it, there has been a nonstop harangue encouraging Christians to get involved in politics—mostly by contributing money. The money is supposedly to help those same evangelists send a message to Washington. Unfortunately, the message sent is not the beautiful simple message of God's love expressed in Christ. The Gospel cannot compete, at least in fund-raising terms, with fighting the liberal agenda and other emotionally explosive political issues. Sadly, Christians are much more willing to finance a right-wing political effort than any spiritual one.

It is the same with politics as with so many of the other deadly detours. A great part of the attraction is that a deadly detour offers an easier way to feel righteous. It is always significantly easier to send money to some Christian organization that is promoting a political agenda than it is to do the real work Christ calls us to do. This is especially true when we wholeheartedly agree with that agenda, which almost every Christian intuitively does. Sending money, signing petitions, attending rallies, working on behalf of candidates—all these things make Christians feel that they are productively engaged in God's work. But they are all deadly detours—deadly because they rob us of the joy we receive when we are obedient and particularly because people are dying in their sin while we pursue our political agendas instead of the agenda Christ commands us to pursue.

He is the only cause I'll own
From all others I have flown
Good citizen of earth I'll be

But He *rules the universe for me*
This world is not my home.

As Christians we very much need to bring a scripturally correct focus into our lives here on earth. We need to understand the nature of our residence here and live accordingly. Fortunately, there is a great deal of Scripture to help us with this, and it is very plain and clear. Scripture repeatedly tells us that our citizenship is in heaven, not here. Philippians 3:20–21 says,

> But our citizenship is in heaven. And we eagerly await a Savior from there, the Lord Jesus Christ, who, by the power that enables him to bring everything under his control, will transform our lowly bodies so that they will be like his glorious body.

If our citizenship is elsewhere, what status do we have here on earth? Again, as always, Scripture provides the answer. First Peter 2:11–12 tells us,

> Dear friends, I urge you, as aliens and strangers in this world, to abstain from sinful desires, which war against your soul. Live such good lives among the pagans that, though they accuse you of doing wrong, they may see your good deeds and glorify God on the day he visits us.

Our citizenship is in heaven, and we are aliens and strangers here, instructed to live good lives so that earthly citizens may see our good deeds. Paul, in his second letter to the Corinthians, tells us that Christ has committed his message of reconciliation to us and says in chapter five, verse twenty, "We are therefore Christ's ambassadors, as though God were making his appeal through us." What could be plainer? Nowhere in Scripture are we instructed to try to influence governmental policy or control political power.

> *He is the only cause I'll own*
> *I see Him on his throne*
> *I don't crave majority*
> *I yield to His authority*
> *This world is not my home.*

Instead, we are to recognize that we are aliens and strangers. We are to lead good lives, and we are to convey the message of reconciliation. (When was the last time you heard a sermon urging us to reach out in love to the liberal Democrats?) We are to be ambassadors of the One to whom we belong. It is important to remember that ambassadors do not meddle in the internal affairs of the country to which they are sent. They merely represent the interests and carry the messages of their homeland. It is important to remember that this world is not our home. Like political ambassadors, we have our very specific orders. We are to be salt and light; we are to make disciples; we are to show Jesus high and lifted up, *none* of which has anything to do with controlling the White House or the state house.

This does not mean that we should be oblivious to what is going on around us. This does not mean that we should be anything less than caring, fully informed citizens. We should certainly vote for good people and some of us might even be led to enter political life ourselves. And as a *political* strategy, signing petitions or supporting a candidate is your right as an American citizen. Just do not confuse it with your duty as a Christian. The deadly detour is in making politics more important than our citizenship in heaven and in forgetting the debt of love we owe to Jesus.

(handwritten margin note: don't idolize politics !!! politicize your faith !!! SATANIZE your opposition)

We are, however, not to be oblivious to the evil all around us or to the pain and suffering it causes. Jesus was not oblivious, and we are to emulate him. The deadly detour is our thinking that political power and position are the answers to problems, when in reality only Christ is the answer. The deadliest of the detours, though, is taken when what we do politically, thinking we are being righteous, actually drives people away from Jesus rather than draws them to him. If we ask, regarding any activity in which we are involved, Does what I am doing draw people to the Savior or repel them? Does what I am doing tell people who Jesus is and why he came? Does what I am doing give people reasons to reject Jesus rather than reasons to accept him? Honest answers to these questions prove that most activities related to the so-called Moral Majority and Religious Right do not exemplify Jesus.

We must remember that Christians will never be a majority here. We are God's remnant. We are aliens and strangers on earth. I do not want to be a part of the Religious Right, but I would *love* to be a part of the religious caring, the religious sharing, the religious loving, the religious bringers of salt and light.

> He is the only cause I'll own
> My efforts I will hone
> To show Him high and lifted up
> I'll gladly drink from His dear cup
> This world is not my home.

The Moral Majority and the Religious Right create more heat than light and more bitterness than sweet.

While all Christians would love to see righteous people in places of authority and would love to see biblical ideals espoused in high places, there is some evidence to suggest that the body of Christ is stronger and more robust when it is challenged and threatened. Certainly its most dramatic growth has often been when it has been most vigorously persecuted. This is not to suggest that we should seek or pray for empowerment through persecution and evil. It is, however, to suggest that our agenda, our mandate, and our motivation must remain the same regardless of who is in power in Washington. What we are called to do does not change with control of the White House or Congress. Who controls the reins of power here on earth should not affect or change our mission. We serve an unchanging, ever-constant God and our marching orders are clear and consistent—proclaim the Gospel.

Do we care who our president and other elected officials are? Of course. Should this change our basic modus operandi? It should not. If an administration more sympathetic to Christian values is in power, we should be thankful but be just as diligent about our Master's business. Is it not ironic that even with a Republican administration for twelve years, divorce rates still climbed, alcoholism and drug traffic increased, pornography was openly peddled, and other evils prospered? We can never expect a political agenda to heal the land. Only the Gospel can do that. We need to present Jesus high and lifted up. We need to be salt and light. We need to be ambassadors. We need to be making disciples. When an administration is in power that we perceive to be unsympathetic to Christian values, what should we do? *Exactly the same thing.* Our mission does not change. We do not suddenly get new marching orders that call for us to organize politically and put our time and God's money toward an attempt to unseat the new unsympathetic regime. No. Sin, death, and hell remain the same. Jesus' saving power remains the same. The gospel message remains the same. Our task remains the same. The occupant of the White House remains relatively unimportant in the eternal scheme of things. What remains desperately important is the fact that without a saving knowledge of Jesus; men, women, boys, and girls are lost eternally.

He is the only cause I'll own
The best seed must be sown
For life throughout eternity
He is the only certainty
This world is not my home.

Christians must understand and act on what Scripture says about the sweep of history. The Bible tells us that things will inevitably get worse until Jesus comes again. The best we can do is to retard the growth of evil by being the salt we are admonished to be in the Sermon on the Mount. And the way to be salt is by showing the relevance of Christ to all of life—to the issues of the day. It is also important to know that the only reason to be the preservative salt is so that more men and women can be told about who Jesus is and why he came; it is to preserve more opportunities to show him high and lifted up. To think that we can change the course of history through politics is folly. To think that we can change the hearts of men by anything other than Christ is blasphemy. Let us be sure that we know what we are doing and why we are doing it. Let us not worry about being politically correct. Let us worry about being biblically correct.

As our most visible Christian leaders pursue a political agenda, a number of things happen—almost all of which are bad. The first thing that happens is that the discourse between them and the world focuses on anything except Jesus and why he came. Syndicated newspaper columns, radio and television talk shows, and, increasingly, letters to the editors of important newspapers focus on the politics of Christians rather than the message of Christ. This should not be, and it is not the kind of dialogue we should want. We should want dialogue that gives us the opportunity to graciously bring biblical truth to bear on current topics and that shows the relevance of Jesus to all of life. At the very best, the time given to politics is time taken away from proclaiming the Gospel. For Christians, political activism, regardless of how noble its goals, is a deadly detour.

He is the only cause I'll own
He is the cornerstone
He is the One to right the wrong
In Him alone I will be strong
This world is not my home.

He is the cornerstone

He is the One to right the wrong
In Him alone I will be strong
This world is not my home.

FOUR
Deadly Detour #3:
Thwarting
the Homosexual Agenda

Three of my close friends have died of AIDS. One of them was the great tennis star, Arthur Ashe, who contracted the disease from a blood transfusion during heart surgery. The other two were colleagues in my company. Only one of them was a homosexual. Even though only one was a homosexual, and was deep in the closet until AIDS forced him to ask for help, my association with these three friends with AIDS has brought me into more contact with homosexuals during the past few years than in all of the previous years of my life. Even now, as I try to serve in causes that were important to my friend Arthur Ashe, I am meeting more and more openly homosexual people, even though Arthur's interest was to defeat AIDS, not to promote the so-called homosexual agenda.

Even with this vastly increased contact with homosexuals, I am far from being an expert on homosexuality. However, from empirical evidence (homosexuals whom I have personally known and known about), I am sure of one thing: the term *gay* is one of the least accurate words you could possibly apply to homosexuals as a group. To use the word *gay* is a cruel joke, one they seem to want to play on themselves. The reality that I have experienced with homosexuals is that they are both individually and as a group among the saddest, most troubled, most torn, and most miserable people around.

Even in loud militancy, even in extreme stridency, even in the most blatant vulgar exhibitionism, even in the most forced revelry, there is a sadness just below the surface of all homosexuals that I think discerning people, particularly discerning Christians, should see. I am fully aware that they publicly and vehemently deny this and that they increasingly and loudly proclaim a sense of joy and pride in who they are and what they do. I do not believe it. *Every* homosexual with whom I have had private conversations, in a trusting relationship, has let me know how troubled and uncomfortable they are with their homosexuality. I do not believe that my experiences are unique. I do believe, perhaps naïvely, that their sense of hopelessness causes the most bizarre, promiscuous, and confrontational kind of behavior. They see no possibility either of change or of a life of righteousness, so they proceed full speed ahead in an effort to justify themselves and their behavior.

In addition, many homosexuals have another strong reason to be dismayed. The way in which society generally, and the church particularly, has treated them should cause concern and sorrow to all involved. If the church would treat homosexuals with compassion, as persons of great worth because Jesus died for them, it would be so much easier for homosexuals to see themselves in the light of biblical truth. But as long as the church treats them as inherently reprehensible, homosexuals justify their belief that homosexuality is not their sin, their problem—the way they are viewed and treated is the problem.

While we can be thankful for a few effective, growing ministries to homosexuals such as Exodus International, there is still much ignorance. It should come as no surprise that the church, when confronted (and that is the right word) with more and more openly homosexual people and with more and more blatant homosexual activity and with more and more strident homosexual demands, has no adequate response.

Unfortunately and tragically, the response that the church has had has been terribly flawed in one of two ways. We have, in absolute disregard of biblical truth, either accepted homosexual *behavior* and practice as being compatible with God's laws, or we have presented a picture of homosexuals that has evoked absolute loathing and revulsion toward them as people. Both are equally bad and equally wrong. Both are deadly detours.

In its search for an understanding of homosexuality, the church has gone down a great number of unproductive side roads. Some churches have accepted monogamous homosexual behavior. Some have said that there is no such thing and have not accepted any kind of homosexual activity as normal. Both practices eventually lead to questions of homosexual marriages and to homosexual clergy. All are the deadliest of detours.

The church has too often allowed itself to be dragged into questions about how a person becomes a homosexual. Is homosexuality genetically acquired or environmentally produced? Then come more questions: Can they be cured? Can they, through their own wills, or with counseling, or through prayer, or by a miraculous touch from God, be delivered from homosexuality? Can they change? Finally, the church asks perhaps the most inflammatory question of all: Is AIDS God's punishment for homosexuals? As interesting as these questions are, they are basically deadly detours for the church. They are deadly detours because the purpose of exploring them is to determine whether or not homosexual activity is sinful. We already have that answer. If, however, finding the answers to these questions will help to better understand homosexuals, to better minister to them, and to better point them to the person of Jesus, then the questions merit the best possible thinking by our very best scholars.

Far too many of the churches that have flatly stated that any kind of homosexual activity is sinful, antibiblical, and can never be condoned have tailored their response to show how vile, loathsome, and repugnant homosexual behavior *and* homosexuals themselves are. It is among this group of Christians that we hear the most about the secret and sinister "homosexual agenda."

Of course, to fight the homosexual agenda, every Christian needs to sign a petition and send a financial contribution to our highly visible church leaders who are the only ones standing between us and these filthy, disease-ridden subhumans whose agenda is to take over America and hijack all our children into a life of sodomy. For this to be the primary public message on homosexuality by so-called Bible-believing churches is a heartbreaking travesty.

The church has once again allowed itself to be co-opted by the politicians. The issues of homosexuals and the military, and the public school curricula, and civil rights, and so forth, which politicians of *both* left and right are using for their own ends, are deadly detours for the church. While these issues are fodder for interesting debates, they have little to do with the first things of the Gospel, little to do with what we as Christians are uniquely and peculiarly called to do, little to do with the fact that Jesus is right for *whatever* is wrong in your life, and little to do with his kingdom.

It seems to me that what is most lacking in this deadly detour taken by the church is compassion. We have evoked almost every possible emotion from intellectual curiosity to revulsion where homosexuals are concerned. But we have evoked almost no compassion. Do not confuse weak, patronizing, antibiblical acceptance of sinful behavior with the kind of genuine compassion that will not rest until the first things of the Gospel are presented. True compassion is presenting the first things of the Gospel because one cannot bear to think of a particular person's spending eternity in hell.

Just as bad as the hate mongers, who have found the homosexual agenda to be a wonderful scare tactic (read fundraising tactic), are Christians who excuse any kind of homosexual activity in the name of brotherhood and acceptance. The poor homosexuals—one branch of the church tells them that they are worse than scum, while the other tells them that they are perfectly all right just as they are. There is neither real Christian compassion nor the real gospel message in either church. Both have taken deadly detours with hell as the destination.

There are some principles, however, that I believe are absolutely biblical. And if Christians are to be obedient to our calling where homosexuals are concerned, then we must adhere to those principles. Please consider them carefully:

1. Homosexuals are people for whom Christ died.
2. Homosexuals deserve the opportunity to have the claims of Christ presented to them in a clear, loving way as much as anyone else.
3. Homosexual acts are sinful and cannot be condoned, but in eternal terms, they are no worse than any other sins. *Any* sin that is not forgiven, not covered by the blood of Jesus is utterly vile to a holy God and is cause for eternal punishment.
4. How people *become* homosexuals is of academic interest, but it is in no way central to the work of the church where homosexuals are concerned.
5. The number of Americans who *are* homosexual, whether it is 1 percent or 10 percent of the population, is an interesting sociological and demographic question, but it should have nothing to do with the church's response to homosexuals.
6. Whether or not AIDS is God's judgment on homosexuals is an interesting academic and theological question, but it is in no way central to the work of the church where homosexuals and/or AIDS victims are concerned.
7. As responsible parents, citizens, and Christians, we need to be concerned about our public schools, about fairness for all our fellow citizens, about our military, and about all the other components of a democratic society.

As Christians, however, our first allegiance is to our Lord Jesus Christ and to his kingdom. If we biblically and consistently integrate our faith into all of life, we will not see any conflict between what the Bible teaches and the way we live. If we consciously overlay all our interests, concerns, and cares with the facts that Jesus came, his kingdom is not of this world, and he is right for whatever is wrong in life, then we will love the sinner but hate the sin. We will love the homosexual but hate homosexuality. In this way we will not have taken the deadly homosexual-agenda detour.

The church is busy, as it should be, with all kinds of strategies to reach the world. An example is Co Mission, an organization designed to bring huge quantities of Christian resources to bear on Eastern Europe and the former Soviet Union. This effort is producing a degree of cooperation among individual Christians, churches, and para-church organizations that is unprecedented. Another example is Charles Colson and his wonderfully effective Prison Fellowship, which has almost universal support among evangelical Christians.

These are just two examples of high-profile ministries currently enjoying massive support from God's people in America. They are both terrific, as are many other very worthwhile and effective ministries. However, is it not ironic and does it not seem strange that American Christians can engender such enthusiasm for ministries to former enemies thousands of miles away? Is it not ironic and does it not seem strange that we support a ministry to convicted criminals guilty of every kind of crime from mass murder, to rape, to child molestation, to armed robbery, to all kinds of white-collar crime? Yet, we have almost no enthusiasm for ministering to a group of people who live with us and work with us but who are not only dying in their sins by the thousands every week but also, while they live, are existing in a kind of surreal world that is a foretaste of the hell to which the church is assigning them.

It is important that we acknowledge with gratitude and admiration the small, courageous ministries to homosexuals that exist but for the most part labor in underfunded obscurity. Among the most effective of these are Exodus International, the Olive Branch, and Mel Trotter Ministries. These efforts, however, are minuscule, vis-à-vis the size of the task and the proximity of those who need to be reached. This is because it is much easier and more glamorous to spend two weeks in the Ukraine handing out tracts or to support a respected person such as Chuck Colson in his prison ministry than it is to do the tough, gritty, decidedly unglamorous work of befriending a homosexual, building a relationship of trust, and presenting the claims of Christ. As fallen people, our natural instinct is always to look for the broad, easy, downhill path, which is, at best, a detour and, at worst, a *deadly* detour. Any path that keeps us from ministering to the homosexuals around us is a deadly detour indeed.

While we do not minister to homosexuals, we do not ignore them either. Our televangelists increase their fund-raising take by showing the worst pictures of homosexuals they can get their hands on. In highly publicized forums, denominations debate the causes of homosexuality. As usual, we spend much time counting and keeping score and wringing our hands about the actual number of homosexuals. We are overly concerned about the percentage of the population they comprise, as if that matters very much when we reach out to only a tiny fraction of the ones that we know exist. The right wing of the church exercises itself over how best to fight the homosexual agenda while the left wing of the church, in a blatant departure from biblical truth, tells them: "You're okay. Come on in. Your vile practices are accepted here." Deadly, deadly detours. The homosexuals die and go to an eternal hell.

Where are the great evangelical Christian leaders? Where are the evangelical denominations? Where are the highly organized para-church organizations? Where are the Co Mission-type efforts to present Jesus in all his beauty, majesty, power, glory, and *compassion* to homosexuals? Where is the Chuck Colson to lead an effort to reach this poor, needy, dying group of people? How does the church get off this deadly detour? Thankfully, there are exits vis-à-vis homosexuals. As always, the Bible plainly points the way. As always, the heavenly highway is not a wide, easy, downhill path. It is narrow, steep, rocky, and dangerous; but it leads to joy, blessing, and the eternal, "Well done."

As I have learned in a small way, the heavenly highway in regard to homosexuals is narrowest, steepest, rockiest, and most dangerous when you walk it, not with some largely abstract, largely faceless group, but when you walk it with a person you know and care about. Although the church *must* begin to develop and implement, in a massive strategic way, a plan to reach homosexuals as a group, the effort must begin with individual Christians—where our contacts with homosexuals are the closest and most personal.

Many people have many reasons to be thankful for the faithful ministry of Dr. Richard C. Halverson. As the former chaplain for the United States Senate and for many years prior to that as the pastor of four significant churches, Dr. Halverson has been a most effective minister of God's Word. Even though I live a long way from Washington, Dr. Halverson ministers to me via his biweekly devotional letter "Perspective."

In the June 9, 1993, edition of "Perspective," Dr. Halverson has a powerful word for those who have that steepest of roads to walk, the one we are called to walk when our own child is a homosexual. Because it represents such a brilliant signpost on the heavenly highway and is so pointedly pertinent to our message, I am, with Dr. Halverson's permission, quoting his brief letter in its entirety.

> Dear Friend:
>
> Through the years as a pastor of four churches (in Missouri, California, and Maryland), it was *my responsibility (and privilege) to minister to those who were homosexual.* [All the emphasis in the letter are Dr. Halverson's. I cannot help but comment here about the impact and potency of his use of the phrase "and privilege" when he begins to tell of his ministry to homosexuals. May more of us understand that it would be a privilege to present Jesus to homosexuals!]
>
> Based upon this experience, let me share *how I would respond to a child of mine* who discovered that he/she was homosexual . . .
>
> First, and most importantly, *I would not cease loving them,* or love them less than before they shared their situation with me.
>
> As a matter of fact, I would *love them more than ever,* if that were possible.
>
> They would have my hearing—*as often and as long as they wanted to discuss the matter* with me.

I would do my best *not to be judgmental!*

I would not treat them as "queer" or whatever other designation is a "put down."

I would do all I could to *persuade them to be chaste* (just as I would a heterosexual child before marriage).

I would remind them with all the wisdom God gives me, that *He loves them,* that *He understands them,* that *His love is unconditional and everlasting.*

I would urge their *total commitment to Jesus Christ,* that He might change them—as He transformed my life from a pleasure loving playboy, and as He transformed many others to be His obedient servants—to conform to His perfect plan for their lives.

I would do all in my power—and with love— *to try and dissuade them from adopting a homosexual lifestyle.*

I would remind them that Christ created them for Himself, and they could become themselves, only as they gave themselves to Him that He might rule in their bodies. (Colossians 1:16, 27–29; 2:9–10; Romans 12:1–2) " . . . know ye not that your body is the temple of the Holy Spirit . . ." (1 Corinthians 6:19).

Grace and Peace,
Richard C. Halverson

Wow! Powerful! Perfect! Potent! This says it all.

While Dr. Halverson's wonderful letter deals specifically with a parent-child relationship, its truths are so universal that they can be applied to every Christian's relationship with every nonbelieving homosexual; thus becoming the basis for our ministry to them.

Every evangelical Christian should have a copy of Dr. Halverson's principles. Every time he or she gets a letter seeking funds to fight the homosexual agenda, a copy of Dr. Halverson's principles should be sent in reply with a note stating: "This is my homosexual agenda. I believe it is the biblical homosexual agenda. I urge you and your organization to help in reaching out to homosexuals in a loving way so that they may know the loving, transforming, saving power of Jesus Christ, who loves them and died for them."

Every Christian church and every para-church group must develop a more effective, biblically based, homosexual agenda. We cannot continue to allow the church to take the deadly detours of antibiblical acceptance of homosexual practices, the reviling of homosexuals themselves, or the side roads of the politicians. We must constantly remind ourselves of the first things of the Gospel, that Jesus came, that his kingdom is not of this world, that we have a special specific and peculiar responsibility, and that Jesus is right for whatever is wrong with our lives. This should be the only heavenly highway where homosexuals are concerned. We must begin the journey now.

FIVE

DEADLY DETOUR #4:
FIGHTING
OTHER CHRISTIANS
OVER DOCTRINAL PURITY

When Chuck Swindoll, a prominent and respected evangelical pastor, radio teacher, and writer accepted the call to become president of Dallas Theological Seminary, it should have been a very big story in the metroplex media. It barely made a small back-page ripple in the *Dallas Morning News* and was completely ignored by television. When Russell Dilday was fired in an abrupt and unseemly way from the presidency of Southwestern Theological Seminary in Ft. Worth, it created a media feeding frenzy. Both the Dallas and the Ft. Worth papers carried front-page stories on the firing for several days, and the local television stations interviewed everyone who was even remotely connected to the event.

Swindoll's associating with the seminary in Dallas should have been a bigger story. The long-range ramifications are much more significant. The Swindoll-Dallas Seminary story, however, had none of the bitter Christian infighting that the media finds so intriguing and so juicy.

The way that the Dallas-Ft. Worth media played out these two stories should be very instructive for Christians. The lesson is that the world will always be much more interested in and fascinated by that which shows Christians to be less than we claim to be than it is in that which shows Christians transformed by the power of the Gospel. The reason for this is very simple and is as old as the Gospel itself. When Christians fail, fight, and fall, non-Christians acquire another excuse to reject the claims of Christ. They quite easily and quite logically say, "See, there is really nothing to this Christianity business. I get enough fighting, bickering, and back-biting without getting into that mess." The fact that they are really rejecting imperfect Christians rather than the perfect Jesus is a distinction too subtle to ask them to make. It is a distinction they should not have to make. If we Christians properly held up our end, all that the world would be able to say is, "Behold, how they love one another!"

Sadly, this exclamation-producing love is seen far too seldom by the world. When the world takes note of Christians at all, it is almost always brought about by our rivalries—by the things that drive us apart—rather than by our love for one another and our commitment to the Savior. For the most part, the fighting that the world sees is about issues they care little about and words they do not understand. *Inerrancy, dispensationalism, glossolalia, imputation, infusion, pre-* and *postmillennialism* are words that represent issues that are very difficult for the world to understand or get very excited about. While we debate them, fight over them, and split over them, the people out in the real word are grappling with more urgent problems that are literally dragging them down to death and hell.

In addition to the terribly negative influence that public brawls among Christians have on non-Christians, it is important to note that all the time, energy, and money that go into these fights are resources that are unavailable for the primary tasks we are commanded by our Lord Jesus to do. When we are engaged in these contests, we are not being the salt we are commanded to be, we are not making disciples, we are not showing Jesus high and lifted up. When we are fighting, we are not winning.

None of the above is meant to say that theology and doctrine are unimportant. They are terribly important. Scripture commands us to study so as to correctly understand and then be able to explain the hope that is within us. The great success of the early church and the preaching of the apostles was in large measure due to their understanding and use of Scripture to prove both the divinity of Jesus and his messianic claims. Most of Paul's writing was doctrinal in nature, and if we do not, as Swindoll says, care about doctrine and theology, we are on the way to cultism. It is only Scripture, and its correct interpretation, that keeps us from falling into all kinds of grievous and deadly errors. As Protestants, products of the Reformation, we believe wholeheartedly in *sola scriptura*— scripture alone—as *the* authority for all we do and all we believe. We *must* care deeply about what it says to us.

Our problem is not in studying too much or in caring too much about even the most minute detail of doctrine. Our problem is in our priorities, in our methodology, and in our behavior. Someone has said, "When everyone has heard who Jesus is and why he came, maybe then I will feel like debating the finer points of theology. Until then, I just don't have the time." In fact, the successful para-church organizations have prioritized their ministries with this in mind. Campus Crusade, Young Life, the Navigators, and so forth, concentrate on presenting Jesus as Savior and Lord and ask that a decision be made about him. They have their priorities in order. And, before any one of us can afford to put too much of our time into debating with other Christians about the finer points of theology and doctrine, we must be sure that we are carrying out the minimal command to all Christians—the Great Commission. We do not have a choice if we are to honor Christ. Every Christian is to be salt. Every Christian is to make disciples. After that, we can become involved in the debates and discussions about the finer points of doctrine. But for most Christians, if we are obedient, if we are truly being salt and light, we will have very little time, energy, or enthusiasm for rivalries. We will be so exhilarated by the rest of the contests, the real battles for the eternal souls of men and women, that we will find almost no interest in rivalries between and among our brothers and sisters in Christ.

Nowhere in Scripture are we directly commanded to go out and convince people of the truth of predestination or the falsity of the ordination of women. These and other doctrinal topics are interesting and important, but we should get to them only after we are sure that we have put in the requisite time fulfilling Christ's clear, direct, and unequivocal commands to us. We must keep our priorities straight.

And, if we do become involved in debates about theology, doctrine, and polity, it is most important that we, *and any of those we support*, understand the Christian, scriptural way in which to be involved. First, doctrinal debates are matters for the household of faith. They are, by their very nature, things of concern to Christians. As much as possible, these discussions and debates should be kept inside the church. Real damage to the cause of Christ is done when Christians try to win by using the secular media. Snappy press releases and clever sound bytes may be all right for the world's politicians, but they are not the way in which brothers and sisters in Christ should try to come to mutual understandings about the things of God. Private, low-key, cogent, *prayerful* discussion is surely the only profitable way in which these matters should be discussed. When we air theological debates in the secular press, we are most certainly casting pearls before swine. The world has no interest in our debates. They only see the rancor of the debaters, *not* their love for one another, which is too often either not evident or not there. Christians should not get involved in public debates and confrontations with other Christians. These activities only bring reproach to the cause of Christ. This is a deadly detour.

One of the great enigmas of the twentieth century is how men and women united in their love for and belief in Jesus can become such vociferous and rancorous enemies of one another over theological, doctrinal, or polity issues. Typically, Christians treat worldly people, those with whom they have the

FIGHTING OTHER CHRISTIANS OVER DOCTRINAL PURITY

most fundamental differences, with more courtesy, kindness, and consideration than they do those in the church with whom they disagree. This is not right. It does not please God. It is a deadly detour.

It has always amazed me how people in the world can handle their disagreements so much better than we Christians can handle ours. People in the world often have the most fundamental differences about business issues, yet they do not break fellowship. It often amazes Christians (and I hope convicts us) when we hear that many U.S. congressmen and senators, though from different parties and totally different political perspectives, debate the issues with fire and passion, yet are warm social friends with great personal respect for one another.

In the early days of professional tennis, many issues in the sport involving many millions of dollars were settled in often very heated debates. On one occasion in the Westbury Hotel in London, during the great Wimbledon tournament of 1975, I witnessed two men involved in one of the most intense, vitriolic arguments filled with some of the vilest language I have ever heard. They went toe-to-toe and head-to-head with one another for well over an hour. At that point, one looked at his watch, held up his hand signaling a brief time-out, and very amiably said to the other, "It's about time for the matches to start. Want to share a car out to Wimbledon together?" The other said, "Sure." They recessed their argument and went together to watch tennis—the subject they were debating.

I have almost never seen the equivalent of the friendly legislators or the tennis debaters in a church disagreement. For some perverse, sinful reason, when there are disagreements and debates among Christians, they almost always result in personal rancor and broken fellowship. Why is this? I do not know, but I am sure it is not God honoring or kingdom building. It is a deadly detour.

We must learn to exhibit genuine courtesy, kindness, and consideration toward other Christians with whom we disagree on even major issues. We must learn to love and to show that love. We must learn how to behave ourselves as Christians—especially toward one another. We must learn to be caring, loving friends even with those with whom we have the most major differences.

When I think about Christians and our strong attraction to rivalries, I think of my father-in-law, who spent his whole life in service to God as a pastor and district superintendent of a small, very conservative denomination. The angriest I ever saw him was over the issue of a "divided chancel." Some churches in his denomination either put in, or contemplated putting in, a divided chancel. Fighting that through preaching against it became a focal point of his ministry. He ministered in small oil and agriculture communities of western Pennsylvania. Do you think that those men who worked for Pennzoil or Quaker State or those who were trying to make the hilly farms support a family cared very much about the divided-chancel issue? My father-in-law was both a very intelligent man and a dedicated pastor and churchman. He had to know that the people of western Pennsylvania had more pressing spiritual concerns than whether or not their church had a divided chancel. Yet, that issue occupied much of his time and energy in the later years of his ministry.

Why are we as Christians so attracted to and energized by these peripheral causes? For the same reason as every deadly detour. We take deadly detours because they make us feel active and engaged. They convince us that we are on the front lines of the battle without having to actually be where the real battle is being fought. No matter what the cause might be, no matter how rigorous it might be, no matter how important it might be, it is never as important as the only battle that ultimately counts, which is the battle for the souls of men and women. Their eternal destiny is at stake. When you enter that fray, you know that the forces of evil will be arrayed against you, fighting you every step of the way. You know that to be successful it will be necessary to be out there in the world, out where the needy people are, and out where sin is rampant and powerful. But you can also know that that is where the deadly detour ends, and you can know that as you seek to walk in obedience, the Holy Spirit will guide you. You can rely on God's promises of protection. He does not promise ease and freedom from conflict and persecution. But he does promise to see us through to ultimate victory. And he does promise the joy that comes from faithfully serving on the real front lines of the only battle that matters.

Avoid the deadly detours. Be obedient. Be truly victorious in him.

SIX

DEADLY DETOUR #5:
SHUTTING DOWN
THE ABORTION CLINIC

It is not an exaggeration to say that the abortion issue, and all it involves, presents a greater peril to the church of Jesus Christ in America than any issue since slavery. The absolute horror of the act itself, its proliferation throughout all strata of society, the protection given it by the law, and the church's seeming inability to act in any meaningful, cogent, scripturally cohesive way has been terribly damaging. The church has been unable to mount any effective social or legal response to what can only be called wanton mass murder. But of even greater concern is the frightening reality that the church's ability to do what it was founded to do—make Jesus Christ known—is being seriously impaired. In fact, the way in which the church has responded to abortion has damaged its ability to present the Savior in all his beauty and winsomeness. With the abortion issue, the church has become impotent both legally and socially. It has lost its spiritual high ground because the church's response to the violent crime that abortion is has been violent and criminal.

At this time of great peril for the church, the voices of its leadership seem to be strangely muted, almost eerily quiet. When the evangelical church in America desperately needs a clear, strong, consistent voice bringing scriptural absolutes to bear on the subject of abortion, the silence is, as they say, deafening. Our evangelical leaders are talking and writing about many things, but the battle against abortion does not seem to be one of them.

Without the leadership of our great Bible teachers, antiabortion leadership has fallen to zealous men and women who seem, for the most part, to have forgotten the first things of the Gospel. Thus, we have the unholy spectacle of a mighty effort going forward in Jesus' name with none of his principles or priorities involved. Added to this, we have unseemly conflict among the antiabortion forces. These conflicts are so intense that I am afraid that we might soon see various wings of the antiabortion movement picketing each other as well as the abortion clinics. The church suffers, and again we are on a deadly detour.

It is easy to see how the church took this deadly detour. The horror and heartbreak of the thousands of daily abortions has become so intense for those on the antiabortion front lines that they have become shell shocked. They cracked, because after awhile nothing mattered to them except their stopping the abortions. Any means were justified by this noble end, and carried to its ultimate end, an Operation Rescue zealot murdered an abortion doctor. It is all understandable but tragic. Deadly.

A young, handsome, gifted, seminary-trained pastor was sent into our town, supported by his denomination, to be a church planter. He met with success and had a small, but growing congregation—a viable church was coming together under his leadership. He was energetic and soon, with the support of his congregation, began to be active in the antiabortion movement in our area. Before long almost every sermon that he preached was an antiabortion sermon, every outside speaker came from Operation Rescue or a similar organization. People in the congregation had to demonstrate a comparable commitment to the antiabortion effort or they were made to feel unwelcome. Many families who had provided leadership and funds for the new church left to find a more well-rounded spiritual home. Before too long, only a handful of people who blindly followed the charismatic young leader were left. The normal ongoing work of the church became less and less important as the antiabortion demands on the pastor grew. He was always on the picket lines, was arrested several times, and spent time in jail. He was, and is, a hero to some.

The tragedy is that several years of work by dozens of Christians and tens of thousands of the Lord's dollars were put into the effort to build the church, which now no longer exists—a casualty of the antiabortion effort. That church was planted to make Jesus known, to tell the community why he came, to have people sing the song, "Jesus Is Right for Whatever's Wrong in Your Life." The gospel message has been silenced in that place. A pastor forgot the first things of the gospel. The church in general, and his denomination in particular, are now associated in the minds of the town's citizens, not with Jesus and his power to change lives and prepare people for an eternity with him, but with pickets, marches, police paddy wagons, court hearings, television sound bytes, pushing, shoving, and scuffles—all in the name of a good cause but not in the name of the best cause. Every time we forget the best cause, or put it second, we take a deadly detour.

Obviously, the future holds many questions and many uncertainties for the church relative to the fight against abortion. Just as obviously, however, God has already given us answers.

To me, one of the obvious answers for the church is that both what we are doing and what we are not doing are wrong. We need a drastic change in the church's response to the abortion dilemma. The *Minneapolis Star Tribune* took identical polls, four years apart, of 1001 Minnesota residents. They found that peoples' attitudes on abortion remained virtually unchanged. In spite of all the marches; sit-ins; sensational placards, pamphlets, speeches, and mailings; in spite of an antiabortion president being replaced with a proabortion one; in spite of some Supreme Court victories and some losses; in spite of abortion clinics being vandalized and even burned; in spite of the murder of a doctor who performed abortions; in spite of it all, attitudes had not changed.

Anna Quindlen, the Pulitzer prize winning *New York Times* columnist wrote in frustration about all the abortion activities, pro and con: "They are wasting their time and ours. The venue is not the streets or even the womb. It is the mind." She is only partly correct. Most of the rhetoric and the demonstrations have been a waste of time. But the venue is not the mind. It is the heart. And Jesus is the only One who changes hearts (Jesus is right for whatever is wrong in your life). We have been waging war without our only real weapon—Jesus.

We have even forgotten the words to the old song: "Onward, Christian soldiers, marching as to war, with the cross of Jesus going on before." The cross of Jesus and the Jesus of the cross have been almost entirely absent from the abortion fray. He is nowhere to be seen in angry demonstrations, shouting and shoving matches, church-service disruptions, vandalism, arson, and murder. All of these activities are decidedly of this world. His kingdom emphatically is not.

The insightful question for those in the antiabortion fight who claim the name of Jesus to ask themselves is, Is the effort to save unborn babies worth it if it causes those on either side to lose their souls? This is a very, very tough question to ask. But if we believe the Bible, if we believe the gospel message, if we believe in a kingdom not of this world, if we believe in an eternal heaven and hell, if we believe that we should fear for the soul much more than for the body, *if we believe what Jesus told us,* then the answer is no, the loss of souls is not worth it. If we are in danger of losing souls, then we should remove ourselves completely from any activity that would drive people away from eternal salvation, even if it means losing physical lives here on earth.

Fortunately, and praise God, the best way to save unborn babies and the best way to save souls are not mutually exclusive. In fact, they are one and the same—Jesus is right for whatever is wrong in your life. We somehow missed the truth of Jesus at the beginning of the antiabortion effort, and it has been a disaster, a deadly detour.

One of the things of which we can be certain is that the spiritual rules of engagement between the church and the world, between the church and sin have not changed—even when abortion is the issue. In spite of the horrible attack on innocent lives and in spite of the repugnance that the thought of abortion engenders in the hearts of Christians, the response to the sin of abortion must be the same as the response to any other sin: Jesus.

We have seen abortion as something different, something requiring a special approach, and something given special license. We have said, in effect, that Jesus, the only message we really have when faced with sin, is not good enough, is not effective, and will not work. When we say this, we have already lost the battle, and everyone on both sides loses. If Jesus is not the answer, we do not have an answer.

But Jesus *is* the answer. He is always the only real answer to the sin question.

To date, the antiabortion forces of the church have, in effect, adopted Barry Goldwater's failed 1964 election philosophy: "Extremism in defense of liberty is no vice. . . ." That was wrong then and it is wrong now. The only kind of extremism that Christians should bring to bear on the abortion issue are the extremes inherent in Jesus and his message—lovingkindness, the cup of cold water in his name, going the second mile and giving the second shirt, sacrifice, prayer, and faith.

So far, these extremes have not been much in evidence in our response to abortion. We have approached cannibals, headhunters, and the murderous Auca Indians with the message of a loving, forgiving God personified in Jesus. So far we have been unwilling to use the same approach, the only defensible one we have, with those who favor abortion.

To be sure, the biblical approach to the problem of abortion is much more difficult than the one we are currently following. The heavenly highway is always more difficult than the deadly detour. It is, however, the only way to victory and joy. It is certainly much easier to protest, to be arrested, and even to spend time in jail than it is to commit to the unrelenting demands of an approach that loves people, serves them, and wins them for hearing the claims of Christ. The old show-business adage—dying is easy; it's comedy that's hard—can be contemplated here with benefit. It may seem that marching, protesting, shouting and shoving, and being hauled off to jail are very hard. But compared to a real commitment to follow Jesus, they are easy. We must choose the harder route.

The church's commitment to unborn children will never succeed to the extent it should until it is at least matched by a commitment to those who *are* born. This is where it gets hard, and no facile, overly simplified solutions will fly. Again, Anna Quindlen's writing in the *Times* has some useful insights. She quotes a "rescue woman" on the front lines saying, "If people say they can't afford a baby, we tell them about our warehouse full of clothes and formula." Then Quindlen goes on to comment,

> Ah, if formula were all there was to a baby, babies who grow up to need sneakers, dentists, vegetables, bunk beds, decent homes and love. Last month a teenager who once sat in an abortion clinic for two hours and then walked out and had a baby instead said next time she'd have the abortion. "I love my daughter," she said, "but it's a lot harder than the ladies said at church."

Again, the quick answer is not sufficient. It is difficult if not impossible to adequately respond to this proabortion observation: "Every time pro-lifers go to picket an abortion clinic they drive by several neighborhoods in which there are children who desperately need help. Why don't they stop?" A tough question, but one that those in the church who fight against abortion need to answer.

It has never been tougher to be a child in America. With nearly half of all marriages ending in divorce, the problems for children begin. Child abuse, child pornography, child alcohol and drug addiction, child sexual molestation, and the violent death of children have never been more rampant. Christians in America must at least be as concerned about the bodies and souls of *these* children as we are with the unborn. There are fewer newspaper headlines and television appearances connected with these children's needs, but their needs, particularly their spiritual needs, are just as acute as those of the unborn. The church, if it is to have any credibility on the abortion issue and, more importantly, if it is to obey Scripture, must give these children its urgent attention. Every church that is in any way involved in the antiabortion fight must give at least as much attention to ministering to living children—meeting both their physical needs and helping them to sing "Jesus loves me! this I know, For the Bible tells me so." Jesus does love the little children. We need to make sure not only that they know it but also that they commit their lives to him.

There is also a heavenly highway that leads us to those involved with abortion—the women having them, the doctors performing them, the agencies promoting them. We must see our primary goal not as stopping abortion but as presenting the

Gospel of Jesus Christ. We need to see all those who are involved with abortion as a mission field ripe for harvest for which we ask God to send forth reapers. If we really want to help stop abortion, this is the way, the scriptural way, to begin. The abortion battle is a battle for hearts. For Christians every battle is a battle for hearts. Abortion is no different. Pickets, insults, civil disobedience, harassment, vandalism, and arson will not win the battle for hearts. Jesus Christ, whom we present with persistence, prayer, and lovingkindness is the only hope. Jesus *is* right for whatever is wrong in your life. Abortion is wrong. Jesus is right for it.

The Crisis Pregnancy Center movement, supported by local churches, is perhaps the most effective of the efforts to minister to all those involved with abortion. They present the Gospel along with quality loving care for those most in need. They are a wonderful example of right.

I am usually very cynical about grandiose undertakings as far as the church is concerned. I remember all those times that I have read where some committee or commission or general conference of my own denomination has decreed something or said that we believe this or that. Often I have thought, *Wait a minute, that's not what I believe or what anybody in the church I go to believes.* Official pronouncements are usually not worth the paper on which their press releases are written. Individual Christians and their local churches is where change happens, where it needs to happen. However, the church's involvement with the abortion issue has been such a deadly detour, has gone so far down the wrong road with so little leadership, that this is one time we need to rally "God's army of the meek" in a special way. We need to get our most trusted Bible teachers—Billy

Graham, Chuck Swindoll, Chuck Colson, Charles Stanley, Steve Brown, Bill Hybels, Ray Pritchard, and so forth—together to draft a statement that they can all sign to be read in all Bible-believing churches and on all Bible-teaching broadcasts, calling the church to a scriptural response to abortion.

I hope our leaders will begin to lead us scripturally where abortion is concerned. It is up to each of us individually, however, to respond to God's leading. As always, we must choose either the deadly detour or the heavenly highway. Where abortion is concerned, the heavenly highway is very narrow indeed, and it is a hard path to follow. It is, however, the only way to victory. But, while it is a hard path to follow, it is not dimly lit or hard to find. The directions to it are not arcane or mystical. They are contained in the Sermon on the Mount—in the admonition to be salt and light—and in the Great Commission.

If we want to avoid the deadly detour where abortion is concerned, we need to see that all those who are involved are not any different from any others who have not met Jesus. We need to see them as ones to whom we are called to minister. As individuals, we must become active in and supportive of scripturally obedient organizations such as the Crisis Pregnancy Centers and/or begin our personal evangelistic and discipling efforts among those involved. The Bible provides both strategy and tactics—a heavenly highway. Let us travel it. There is no other way that leads to life.

SEVEN
DEADLY DETOUR #6: CLEANING UP CHRISTIAN TELEVISION

One of these days, the American church must begin to clean up the mess on television. It will take great commitment over a long period of time. It must involve our very best, our most trusted and most talented leaders. It will be very expensive. It must be done with love, even amidst great pain. And, as with anything of any significance, it will take a large measure of God's grace for us to be successful.

We have allowed the television mess to become deeply rooted. To overcome its damaging effect on the true message of Jesus' righteousness and holiness and his call for our commitment to the first things of the Gospel and to building God's kingdom is going to be very, very difficult. But we must begin.

Do not jump to conclusions, though. The television mess that I am talking about has nothing to do with any programming on ABC, CBS, NBC, or PBS. It has nothing to do with HBO, Showtime, Cinemax, or any of the movie channels. It has nothing to do with any of the comedy channels or USA or even what is on the public-access channels. The mess I am referring to is our own. The television mess most damaging to God's kingdom in America is what is known, sadly, as religious television. This is the television mess that needs a new broom, which sweeps clean, applied to it. We made the mess—or at least allowed it to happen—now we must clean it up.

Until there is at least some semblance of order in our own television house, our spending time, energy, and money on the world's television is hypocritical, embarrassing, and counterproductive. It is a deadly detour.

When we think in terms of eternity, about a kingdom not of this world, the most dangerous and potentially damaging television programming that both Christians and non-Christians can see, is not sex and violence but that which deliberately distorts the Gospel, the kind that uses Jesus for personal gain, the kind that when written about appears in the newspaper's legal and crime section.

Both the shoddy and the outright dishonest television programs that first usurp, and then trade on, the excellent name of Jesus, are far more damaging to the mission of the church than even the worst that is produced in Hollywood. It is more damaging because it leaches the salt of the Gospel right out of the soil of society. The salt that Jesus asks each of his disciples to be is the beginning of a foundation for faith. The salt in our lives prepares unbelievers for a fair, at least neutral, hearing for the claims of Christ. Christians, as they work to be salt, help to present a picture of Jesus in his beauty and majesty. Much of so-called religious television washes the salt into a murky stream of dishonesty, deceit, and debacle.

The damage done to the church by the Bakker and Swaggert fiascoes is incalculable. They brought the church into disrepute and held it up to ridicule, making it a joke. When the church becomes a joke, the cause of Christ is much worse off than when it is seriously fought against, because persecution builds the church and strengthens the saints.

In retrospect, the saddest thing about the Bakker and Swaggert disasters is that many discerning Christian leaders knew something was terribly wrong, particularly with the Bakker organization, and did nothing about it. To the contrary, very few turned down invitations to appear on television with Jim and Tammy until the ministry went into free fall. The mess has yet to be fully cleaned up.

The most disgraceful thing about the Bakker and Swaggert sagas is that we seem to have learned little, if anything, from them. Just a cursory look at today's religious-television landscape reveals the same kind of things building back up. The church may not be monitoring the situation, but the major networks are. One has already produced very damaging exposés revealing the same kind of extravagant lifestyles epitomized by Tammy Bakker's air-conditioned Palm Springs dog house. More are planned. Added to the news media's interest is the increasing interest that attorneys general, postal authorities, and law-enforcement officials are showing in the most blatant purveyors of grace for hire.

Even though it may be too late for maximum damage control, it is never too late for us to recognize the problems, avoid the deadly detours, and begin dealing with them in scripturally consistent ways, always remembering that as

Christians we have unique and peculiar responsibilities to present not only the first things of the Gospel but also that Jesus came to establish a kingdom not of this world.

Two of the most consistent and helpful evangelical Christian commentators on religious television in America who have not forsaken the first things of the Gospel are Quentin Schultze, the brilliant writer and teacher at Calvin College in Michigan and Terry Mattingly, who writes the "On Religion" column syndicated weekly by Scripps Howard and who teaches communications at Milligan College in Tennessee.

To be a real roaring lamb (see my book *Roaring Lambs* [Grand Rapids: Zondervan, 1993]), you should read Dr. Schultze's two landmark books, *Redeeming Television* and *Televangelism and American Culture*, both published by Baker Book House. They are must reading for every Christian who wants to understand television and how Christians should relate to it. Then, ask your local newspaper to consistently run Professor Mattingly's column if it is not already doing so. While Dr. Schultze and Professor Mattingly each come at the subject of religious television from slightly different perspectives, both will help you avoid that deadly detour where television is concerned.

Schultze, while scholarly and detailed, is never dull. His forte is analyzing what works and what does not—what television actually delivers and what it fails to deliver. He provides Christians with solid, documented, scholarly information that will help us be discerning, prudent, and good stewards of both our time and God's resources.

Mattingly, is at least as much journalist as academic, and this is reflected in his column. He is more of a critic of content and style than an analyst of numbers and demographics. His sprightly column will make you laugh, cringe, and, if you are a serious Christian, sometimes cry as he helps you consider what goes on in the name of religion on American television.

We can be thankful for both Dr. Schultze and Professor Mattingly. I want to share some of their insights in the next few paragraphs.

As bad as the programs are that distort Scripture and the gospel message in order to generate funds for an obscenely elaborate un-Christian lifestyle, Professor Mattingly helps us see that plain old bad taste and shoddy presentation by even well-meaning Christians on television can be almost as damaging to the cause of Christ. Writing in the magazine *Return to Christian Living* (April, 1993), he tells the story of his friend who is a great fan of religious television. According to Mattingly, long after "pearlygate," his friend still longs for his Jim-and-Tammy-Bakker fix. But, says Mattingly, his friend has other stars to watch and is especially fond of talk shows that feature evangelicals whose hair does not appear to be their own.

Mattingly continues, "Week after week, this media professional turns on his TV and cracks up laughing. He says it would be impossible for secular pros to create satire as cutting-edge as the contents of most religious shows. He calls it 'unintentional comedy.' In his opinion, the electronic church is good precisely because it is so bad." Obviously, this is not the kind of review that thinking, caring, concerned Christians want for religious television in America. Sadly, I am afraid that this is the kind of review most Americans give to Christian television, if they bother to watch at all.

When we get into the question of who watches religious television in America, we need to turn to Dr. Schultze for the answers, which are both revealing and sobering. If we will apply them properly, however, we can avoid television's deadly detour.

In a chapter significantly and ominously titled, "The Evangelistic Myth," from his book, *Televangelism and American Culture*, Dr. Schultze provides us with telling information that many would sooner not have. He makes the following points: (1) religious television in America could not exist without the *billions* (yes, that is billions with a *b*) of dollars that Christians contribute to it *solely* because they believe in its evangelistic outreach and effectiveness; (2) all objective research, however, shows that a belief in televangelism is almost totally misplaced.

First of all, increasingly sophisticated and accurate audience measuring techniques show that the unchurched and unserved are not watching religious television. Dr. Schultze points out that "religious programs are viewed overwhelmingly by churched people who are already quite religious." He cites a *Christianity Today* (December 1, 1980) Gallup poll that found that 85 percent of the viewers of religious broadcasts claim to be already converted. Also, the national ratings information shows that less than 4 percent of the total radio and television audience is reached by religious broadcasts. Taken together, this information gives a clear picture of the tiny percentage of even *potential* respondents to an evangelical message.

Second, and perhaps even more telling, is research that shows how ineffective television (and, indeed almost all mass efforts) is as an instrument of evangelism. Schultze cites a survey (*Christianity Today,* October 16, 1987) done by the Institute for American Church Growth of forty thousand church-related Christians that found that less than .01 percent said they attend church as a result of mass evangelism, including religious radio and television. In stark contrast, more than 85 percent said that they came to Christ and the church primarily through the witness of a friend, relative, or associate.

(Do those figures give you a clue as to where we Christians should be putting our money and our efforts?)

Thus, the evidence is that those who need the evangelistic message are basically not watching, and the small number who do are not moved by the message. Televangelism is both an oxymoron and a deadly detour. It is an oxymoron because evangelism from afar (*tele* means far) does not really happen, and it is a deadly detour because it siphons off desperately needed financial resources and desperately needed personal involvement by Christians in local efforts that really are effective in telling who Jesus is, why he came, and that he is right for everything that is wrong in life.

Here it is important to emphasize that both Terry Mattingly and Quentin Schultze are themselves evangelical Christians, committed to the person of Jesus Christ. They are not nonbelievers standing outside the camp lobbing hand grenades of criticism over the wall. They bring a powerful prophetic message to the church.

While Schultze, Mattingly, and our own critical viewing will show that most so-called religious television falls far below the standard we should expect when the label *Christian* is applied, it is very important to note that a few electronic ministries merit not only our positive attention but also our prayer and financial support.

Most critical observers, both Christians and nonbelievers alike, see Billy Graham's television effort almost totally apart from other so-called televangelists. Graham is unique and will be sorely missed when, inevitably, he passes from the scene. In analyzing Dr. Graham's success, it is impossible not to see his own absolute, personal integrity. From the very earliest days, the Billy Graham Evangelistic Association has seen to it that all that it undertakes is thoroughly, massively bathed in prayer. Weeks, months, and even years before a crusade and its attendant telecasts, thousands of people are praying. (Contrast this with the out-of-the-box, five-day-a-week efforts of most so-called televangelists.) Graham's success lies in his presentation—it is totally scriptural and relatively simple. God honors his Word when it is preached with conviction and sincerity and when it is supported by the prayers of believers.

Longtime Graham watchers and chroniclers of his ministry, however, say his success is not to be measured in the amount of effective evangelism that occurs as a result of his preaching on television. Rather, it is seen in his organization's ability to mobilize and train the churches of a city to do both the more effective personal evangelism and the virtually essential follow-up discipling. The huge arena and stadium events and particularly the telecasts are much more important because they provide the impetus for all the prayer, all the training, all the personal evangelism, and all the follow-up. With this in mind, it is easy to see that Billy Graham is not really a televangelist at all but is a phenomenon of ministry, who deserves our admiration and support. As we contemplate Billy Graham, we do so with great thanksgiving.

Just as Billy Graham should not be seen primarily as a televangelist, the other electronic (radio and television) ministries that merit our support are also not mainly characterized by evangelistic effort. Instead they are much more accurately seen as *teaching ministries* and their leaders as Bible teachers. While the evidence shows that electronic evangelism is almost totally ineffective, electronic teaching, particularly when it moves listeners and viewers to the printed Word to supplement and augment the electronic word, is much more effective and valuable.

Among the radio ministries I cite as examples are Steve Brown's "Key Life" and Chuck Swindoll's "Insight for Living." Both are radio Bible classes and both move listeners to consult the serious and important books authored by the radio teacher as well as the Bible.

As far as a *television* ministry is concerned, I cite Charles Stanley's *In Touch* as an example worthy of consideration. Again, he is basically a teacher of God's Word who also leads viewers to his quality writing. Because his are basically services of worship, without extravagant evangelistic claims, Robert Schuller's *Hour of Power* is worth supporting.

These ministries are offered only as examples and are not intended to be an exhaustive list. The point is that before Christians support any electronic ministries, including the ones just mentioned, it is important to prayerfully consider their worth as instruments for building the kingdom. We all must be tough-minded as we seek to avoid deadly detours. Very few of us have the resources to support even the most worthy ministries, and we must give as the Lord leads us. Those ministries, including our own local churches, one-on-one evangelistic ministries, and proven foreign missions deserve our direct support. After we have considered those and have made an allocation of our tithes and offerings for them, we might then, and only then, consider the most worthy of the electronic ministries.

Both Scripture and our own experience tell us that some people will always be led astray. There will always be wolves among the sheep. It is, however, our responsibility and the responsibility of our Bible teachers to protect as many as possible from the ravages of those who are out to fleece the flock. This protection is more urgently needed in the area of television than in perhaps any other. It is needed to protect naïve Christians and their resources, and it is needed to show the world that neither shoddy programming nor exploitive programming is in any way representative of true Christianity in America.

As I write this book, huge sums of money are being extracted from the wallets and bank accounts of innocents by poor-quality, fraudulent, Christian television programming, which is the only thing representing itself as Christian that many Americans ever see. Even those who do not watch the programs themselves read about them in newspapers and see them "exposed" on the television news magazines. This is the television mess most in need of Christian cleansing.

But how should the cleansing be done? It is almost certain that a public media battle of charges and countercharges is not the way to do it. A circus maximus with Christians fighting Christians is what the forces of evil would most love to see. No, public denunciation and name-calling is not the way to go. Just because the clean-up effort is not public and overt, however, does not mean that it should be less than vigorous.

First, it is very important that true, biblically based electronic ministries distance themselves in every possible way from the false and the shoddy. For the solid, fiscally responsible, Bible-teaching ministries to belong to the same organizations, to come under the same umbrellas as the exploiters of the Gospel is both damaging and confusing to non-Christians as well as the unwary. When quality electronic ministries have even a remote organizational relationship with those espousing false doctrines, the bad ones are lent credibility and legitimacy they in no way deserve.

Before supporting any of even the best electronic ministries, ask them if they belong to religious-broadcasting organizations that also harbor radio and television exploiters. Ask them if they endorse every ministry within the organizations to which they belong. If you do not receive a satisfactory reply, discontinue your support both as a viewer or listener and particularly as a contributor. Let this be your part in helping to clean up the mess.

Second, it is even more important for the true ministries to distance themselves from the false ones by being sure that the delivery system, the network they use to reach viewers, is not one that carries many of the exploitive ones. To have a quality electronic ministry cheek by jowl with a false ministry, and for both of them to be covered by the same network identity, is again both damaging and defeating. It is *much* better for a biblically based, financially responsible ministry to be on a secular station than it is for them to be on a "Christian" delivery system that carries programs of questionable doctrinal and financial purity. If a ministry is not able to broadcast or telecast without using a questionable delivery system, perhaps it should not be on the air at all. Support these ministries that are very careful about the company they keep on the air. Do not support those that associate with those ministries that profane the name and image of Christ in order to be on the air. Avoid the deadly detour. Help clean up the mess.

Third, we must ask our leaders and teachers to begin leading and teaching much more vigorously and consistently where television ministries are concerned. Again, without name-calling or unseemly public battles, the Christian leaders and teachers must let their constituents know what constitutes acceptable electronic ministry and what does not. They must uphold a clear, cogent, biblical standard, admonishing their people to be very careful about watching and supporting questionable ministries. This, of course, must be done with care and discernment, with prayer, and with the leading of the Holy

Spirit. We ask the same kind of quality teaching and leadership on all other subjects, so there is no reason why we should not get it for an area of life as pervasive as television. Chuck Swindoll does this very skillfully, holding up a scriptural standard that his listeners can apply when evaluating both his and other electronic ministries. We need much more of this not only from the electronic media but also from Christian publications and local church pulpits. Our spiritual shepherds must do more in this area to protect the flock from the wolves.

We must also look to our most skillful Christian writers and speakers to help let the world know that many so-called ministries misappropriate the name of Christ and are in no way representative of what true Christians believe and how true Christians act. At key times, such as when the shoddy and profane are in the news, leaders who have won a hearing by their own integrity and accomplishments need to weigh in with guest editorials, op-ed pieces, and other kinds of public statements of true biblical Christianity, using positive examples to expose the negative. This is a way to be salt in the broader popular media. This is the way to avoid television's deadly detour.

So far, we have dealt almost entirely with the negatives, the deadly detours, the mess. There are, of course, heavenly highways to seek out and to follow where television is concerned. They are not cheap or easy, but we should not always be looking for cheap and easy grace. We should look for ways to be obedient and faithful. Nothing of worth to God's kingdom comes without a high price. Jesus set that standard on the cross.

One of the most important heavenly highways we can follow as far as any television programming is concerned is inexpensive. It only takes discernment and discipline. Unfortunately, these two commodities are often in short supply in today's church, but they are desperately needed where television is concerned.

Many social commentators have pointed out that American Christians have the numbers and the power to change the face of television. In a very short time, American Christians could remake television programming. We could do it not by preaching about how bad the programs are, not by protesting, and not by boycotting sponsors. We could do it very simply by watching, and allowing our children to watch, only decent, high-quality, edifying programs. If we Christians in America would watch only quality programs, most of the bad ones would either disappear or be relegated to small cable channels. It is important to recognize that bad programs can only exist if they are supported by great numbers of American Christians. Walt Kelly's cartoon character Pogo made a statement that has never been more appropriate: "We have met the enemy and he is us." We get exactly the kind of programs we support.

So, the first and the most fundamental thing to do is to watch only those programs of real value. If there is nothing on of real value, turn the set off, and leave it off until there is something on that meets those standards. If you do this, even if no one else does, you and your family will be much better off. If others follow, the country will be much better off.

American Christians certainly need to do all we can to change television by controlling what we and our children watch, but we need to do much more than this if we are to use the medium to effectively be salt and light. We need to see the television industry as a mission field and television technology as a powerful means of telling who Jesus is and why he came.

We should be encouraging our best and brightest young people to minister in the television field. God needs his people working in every area of television—writing, acting, direct-ing, producing, and in the business and advertising areas that support those activities—with excellence. Just as Wycliffe and others trained missionaries in the language and culture of dif-ferent tribes and societies, our churches, colleges, and semi-naries need to be training missionaries in the language, culture, and skills of television, so they can go in and help shine the light of the Gospel in its dark places, and allow Jesus to change people one heart at a time. To date, our strategy has been to keep Christians as far away from television as possible and then express outrage at how un-Christian the medium is. The main reason that television almost always gets it wrong where Christians and Christianity is concerned is that they have never seen a real Christian up close on a consistent basis and have never understood the gospel message because no one has ever shared it with them. This must change.

Second and almost equally as important, obedience involves a very deliberate, very proactive effort to produce and distribute high-quality programs that will bring the salt of the Gospel to America. This is a long-range and expensive strategy but a necessary and ultimately rewarding one. We must get both our best creative people and our best business people—people with talent and people with money—to join together in producing the very best possible programs. There should be programs of every genre produced and distributed by Chris-tians—music, drama, comedy, talk shows, documentaries, sports, and so forth. They certainly do not have to be evange-listic or have biblical themes, but they need to be the best they can possibly be—entertaining, informative, and edifying.

Parents, churches, Christian colleges, seminaries, Chris-tian foundations, and para-church organizations must begin to work together where television programs are concerned. Children need to be encouraged to consider careers in television as a ministry. Churches need to begin encouraging a television ministry. Colleges and seminaries need to begin training faculty and developing curriculum to train Christian young people to enter the field. Christian foundations need to begin putting some of their resources behind quality television production and distribution. The para-church organizations need to have a more forceful and more realistic television strategy.

Certainly television presents one of the deadliest detours for American Christians. It is such a dominant part of most of our lives that we can be overcome by it in so many ways. We fall under its evil mesmerizing influence. We allow it to exploit and degrade the God we serve. We dissipate our energies and waste God's resources in vain negative efforts to change it from the outside. But, thankfully, gloriously, God can help his people form a vision of the field of television as a field white unto harvest and to march boldly into that field. His people can also begin to use the communications miracle of television as a means of grace as they produce and distribute godly programming.

Let us get off television's deadly detour for Jesus' sake.

EIGHT
DEADLY DETOUR #7: FIGHTING FOR FAMILY VALUES

Whose family? Whose values?

Every time Christians organize to try to change the world using methods other than those we are biblically commanded to use, we end up spinning our wheels, stymied by clever catch words and phrases. In a pluralistic, multi-cultural society, very few of these clever words and phrases play better than "Whose family? Whose values?" They are potent, catchy, memorable sound bytes and cannot be responded to in kind. Obviously, there is a solid, cogent, biblically correct response, one that answers those questions. The problem is that it takes time and skill to articulate. In a battle of catch phrases and sound bytes, we always lose. This battlefield is no place for us, because when Christians engage in this kind of fight, the essential cause of Christ almost always suffers.

Certainly every Christian knows what the term "family values" means to him or her. Unfortunately, the meaning differs widely even among Christians. So within our own ranks there is no absolute standard to defend, even if mounting a defense in this area were a worthwhile undertaking for Christians. Instead of focusing on and fighting for our individually held values, we need to be defending, by our own positive actions, the absolute, biblical standards of obedience to which we are called.

Even on those very rare occasions when we win a skirmish in the public forum, it hardly matters in terms of eternal victories. The most celebrated of these wins was the famous Dan Quayle versus "Murphy Brown" brouhaha, in which the then vice-president castigated "Murphy Brown," the television sitcom, for glamorizing and glorifying bearing a child out of wedlock. Almost any objective observer would say that the bulk of the country's opinion initially came down on the side of "Murphy Brown." The vice-president, and, by extension, American Christians, were made to look like narrow-minded, humorless, cold-hearted rednecks. The media elite weighed in against family values as espoused by the so-called religious right. In dozens of ways and in many platforms, they asked over and over, "Whose family? Whose values?" It was only when this country's growing illegitimacy rate and all its attendant problems became, for a short time, a big national issue that *The Atlantic*, a prestigious secular publication, handed down its decision trumpeted across its cover: "Dan Quayle Was Right." This was, of course, well after the election was lost by George Bush and Dan Quayle.

The Atlantic's cover did give sermonizers and other family-values advocates and organizations something to cheer about, not to say gloat over, and they were quick to chalk this one up as a win. Well, if this was a victory, it was very hollow and virtually meaningless. Few minds were changed. The illegitimacy rate continued to rise. Christians are still seen by most people in America as narrow-minded, humorless, cold-hearted rednecks. Certainly, there is no evidence to support that, because *The Atlantic declared Dan Quayle a winner, more people know who Jesus is and why he came, that more disciples were made, that ultimate truth prevailed in more hearts and minds. Perhaps a case could be made that some "salt" was applied to the nation's wounded conscience. At best, this was only a small gain for God's kingdom, and the primary costs—in the area of obedience—were enormous. Instead of busying ourselves with obeying Christ's commands, we were able to celebrate and feel righteous because for once, a secular magazine agreed with a position most of us espouse. This is not a major triumph, and again, the price was way too high.*

An even bigger problem for Christians who fight to impose their view of family values on the non-Christian world is that there is almost no empirical high ground to defend. Very sadly, the statistics on one of the most onerous results of poor family values—divorce—show that there is not nearly enough difference in the rates between Christians and non-Christians. In other words, the most potentially damaging attack on the family itself—forget values—is by Christians, who divorce at an ever-increasing rate. It is not intellectually viable to promote our view of family values when we are destroying our own families in the same manner as non-Christians. It might be easy to blame the world for this, saying that even Christians are so inundated by the values of the world that we cannot keep our marriages together and cannot obey biblical principles where our own marriages are concerned. This route would be an attack on the power of the Gospel, on the power of the Holy Spirit to keep and to guide, and on the whole idea that Christians can live triumphantly and obediently in whatever circumstances we find ourselves.

So, before we put our energies and God's resources into battling for our version of family values in non-Christian circles, we need to move with urgency and zeal to strengthen our own Christian families. This is where all the Christian family organizations need to put the vast majority of their efforts. This is where they can be vital and effective. This is where they can shine. When they get distracted by what Hollywood does, by what television networks do, and particularly by political rhetoric, they get lost, beaten down, and are ineffective. I realize it is easier for these organizations to raise funds by making emotional, zealous appeals, promising to use their resources to "thwart the attack on our families by the godless media" or "to send a message to Washington," but this is almost never money well spent. The way it is used almost always generates heat rather than light. It almost never brings about any positive change. It is almost never used to proclaim the gospel message, the only thing that produces genuine, lasting change.

Be discerning. Before contributing to any appeal for funds to fight for family values, ask the key questions: Will my money be used to strengthen Christian families? Will my money be used to proclaim Jesus in a positive, loving, and effective way? If you feel those questions are answered affirmatively, your support might be justified. Avoid those appeals that say, "Let's send a message to Congress [or to Hollywood or to Madison Avenue]." Do not support those that ask for money so your name can be added to a petition to be sent to a government leader, a network head, or an advertising executive. This is about the worst use of Christian dollars imaginable. This kind of petition is rarely taken seriously, is certainly not cost effective, and does not advance God's kingdom. The typical appeal asks us to send $25 or more to support such a petition. Ridiculous. If you feel the need to communicate with someone, you can do it more effectively and more powerfully for the price of a first-class stamp. A sincere, cogent, personal letter speaks much louder than any petition. People receiving such a letter pay attention. It might not change their minds, but it is read, weighed, and considered. Furthermore, in your own personal letter, you can be a discipler by including Scripture that points to Jesus. Petitions from organizations that always send petitions are met with ennui—a yawn.

If we feel called to be a strong advocate for family values, one of the most productive ways to do that is to encourage Christian, family-oriented organizations to concentrate their efforts on Christian families. Urge the leaders of Christian, family-oriented organizations to stay "home" with their work and message. They are desperately needed by Christian families. The world will not hear their message anyway.

A question posed by a Jewish friend in the advertising business raises another very important consideration for Christians who want to be effective and obedient. She asks, "Why is it that from Christians, we hear almost nothing about Christ? We hear about a lot of things from you guys, but almost nothing about this Jesus." When you think about her question and analyze the loudest and most persistent messages from Christians and Christian organizations, you may have to nod your head in agreement with her. From the "Religious Right" the world hears very little about religion. From the Christian Coalition, the world hears very little about Christ. Our real message, the only one that really counts, the one we are commanded to proclaim, the one that says, "Jesus Christ came to save sinners," is lost among the cacophony from those who espouse all sorts of good causes, including the "family values" cause.

As always, we need to focus on our mandate—to proclaim, not to protest. When we are obedient to all that Jesus commanded, we will be so engaged in proclaiming him and making disciples for him that we will have little time for or interest in other causes. The joy that obedience brings will be so satisfying and rewarding that we will become addicted to it and want more. The good news is that joy is there in abundant supply. *Obedience brings joy.*

The rich field to sow with the seeds of the family-values message is that of the Christian family. Because Jesus is already there, messages strengthening the family in biblically sound ways will most often fall on fertile soil, producing fruit. When we go out in the world proclaiming a biblically based family-values message, it falls on the ultimate stony ground, and no real good is done. Without Jesus there, the world will always hit us with the "Whose family? Whose values?" questions. And instead of positive, productive teaching, our message gets lost in rancorous, unproductive debate. Jesus, in all his glory and magnificence, is lost in the fray. When we are sure Jesus has been introduced and is accepted, we can know that the soil has at least been prepared for other discipling messages, including those very vital ones pertaining to God's plan for families.

Some of the most thoughtful Christian writers and thinkers in the area of the family are very concerned with the seeming reluctance of evangelical leaders to speak forthrightly about biblical standards regarding divorce and remarriage. Michael McManus, who has produced excellent writing on the subject, says many church leaders, fearing that they may step on some parishioners' toes, shy away from teaching and preaching that God "hates divorce" (Malachi 2:16). And sermons that emphasize that Jesus did not sanction every remarriage (Matthew 5:32) are even less frequently given. William R. Mattox Jr., the brilliant writer who serves as vice-president for policy at the Family Research Council, says, "Casual attitudes about divorce and remarriage are especially common among Protestants, who have significantly higher rates of marital disruption than Catholics, Jews, or Mormons. This helps to explain why four of the six states with the highest divorce rates—Alabama, Arkansas, Oklahoma, and Tennessee—are found right in the heart of the Bible Belt." Mr. Mattox goes on to say, "While religious leaders do not bear primary responsibility for the absence of public discourse about divorce, they can hardly blame others for the fact that America's divorce problem is greater than that of any other country in the world." Writing in the October 28 edition of *World*, he goes on to cite the very casual attitude of most American churches about performing weddings, about marriage enrichment programs, and about marriage saving programs. His point, and that of Mr. McManus, is that it is more than a little inconsistent for American Christians and our leaders to rage against non-Christians and their view of family, when we seem unwilling to confront very significant problems in our own homes. We desperately need to focus our attention on our own homes and marriages. We need to do this both for the sake of our families and to be the example of righteousness we are called to be. Our family-values efforts need to be directed inward. Anything else is a detour—a deadly one.

Too, Christians who really care about family values will insist that institutions with which they associate and support return to biblical standards where the family is concerned.

Many so-called conservative denominations and Christian colleges proclaim a strong belief in family values, while "winking" at divorce and remarriage without biblical grounds. Many evangelical churches fill their pulpits with divorced and remarried clergy. Many Christian colleges employ divorced and remarried faculty and administrators, never asking about the circumstances surrounding the failed marriage.

Many evangelical churches perform weddings for pregnant women in exactly the same manner as they do for virginal men and women. The rationale is that they want to be supportive and keep the new young family in the church. These young people should be supported, loved, and kept in the church, but the church must not sanction and support unbiblical behavior. This may seem harsh and archaic in these "anything goes" times, but a relaxation of biblical standards among Christians is the greatest of all threats to family values. A cavalier attitude about divorce and extramarital sex among so many churches, Christian colleges, and other Christian organizations inevitably leads to more and more sinful behavior.

The family's biggest problem is not Washington, Hollywood, or Madison Avenue. The biggest danger to the family is Christians failing to take lovingly tough stands for a biblical view of the family in the areas where we have influence. Taking a biblical stance on issues like extramarital sex and divorce and remarriage is never easy. To protest attacks on "family values" by putting a donation on our Master Card is much easier than to live biblically where family issues are concerned.

For more and more Christians, ethically difficult situations are not hypothetical. What do you do when the daughter of a friend in your church wants to have a big traditional wedding in the church, and she is obviously pregnant? What do you do when the most talented and attractive ministerial candidate for the open pulpit in your church is divorced and remarried against scriptural absolutes? What do you do if you serve on the board of a Christian institution and members divorce, remarry, and continue to serve? How do you handle your relationship with a Christian college that seems to have no standard regarding divorce and remarriage for either new or sitting faculty and administrators? Here is an even tougher one for you. How do you handle discord in the marriages of your own children? Is your response, Do whatever makes you happy? In fact, what do you do in your *own* relationships? As a single, do you avoid sexually compromising situations? As a husband or wife, do you love your mate "for better or for worse"? These are the family-values questions with which Christians need to be deeply concerned. This is where Focus On The Family needs to focus. Let's fix our problems before we worry about the state house, the White House, and Congress. Again, Pogo is right: "We have seen the enemy and it is us."

As always, where there is a deadly detour, there is a heavenly highway. Where family values is concerned, the heavenly highway has two parallel lanes, and we need to proceed down both. The first, as we have pointed out, is the need to address the very urgent and persistent problems within Christian families. Our leaders need to speak and teach forcefully and consistently on the need for a strong, deliberate, and decisive return to biblical standards in our own families. In our churches, para-church organizations, and Christian colleges, we must address the rapidly growing problem of divorce. Even when it is painful, even when it strikes close to home, even when it might be unpopular, even when it might be financially costly, we need to be sure that all we do, say, and stand for is biblically sound. This in no way means that we should be anything other than caring and loving toward those whose lives have been shattered by the trauma of divorce. We need to minister to them, love them, and hold them in the body of Christ with all the strength God gives us. However, we cannot overlook sin. We cannot condone unbiblical behavior. We must uphold biblical standards of righteousness in our churches and in our Christian institutions. If the church, para-church organizations, and Christian colleges do not uphold biblical standards, who will? Where can the world look for examples of righteousness?

The other lane on the heavenly highway of family values is the one of service and servanthood offered to non-Christians "that they may see [our] good deeds and praise [our] Father in heaven" (Matthew 5:16). Our helping hand should generally be held out to those non-Christians in need. As he considered this topic, Dr. Ron Sider of Eastern Seminary gave me some wonderful words in this regard:

Few things are more important today than a return to biblical principles and practice in the area of sexuality and the family. Tragically, Christian people who do not know what the Bible teaches too often employ harsh rhetoric and engage in nasty culture wars in a way that repels those who most need to hear our message. They will never listen if they think we hate them. But think of how powerful a different kind of servant witness and wholesome modeling would be. Think of the impact if the first thing radical feminists thought of when the conversation turned to evangelical men was that they had the best reputation for keeping their marriage vows and serving their wives in the costly fashion of Jesus at the cross. Think of the impact if the first thing the homosexual community thought of when someone mentioned evangelicals was that they were the people who lovingly ran the AIDS shelters and tenderly cared for them down to the last gasp. A little consistent wholesome modeling and costly servanthood are worth millions of true words harshly spoken.

Dr. Sider, as he so often does, lays it out very clearly for us. Our most effective efforts in the family-values arena are modeling biblical standards of Christians and reaching out to serve those non-Christians who are hurting most. Raging against Hollywood, Washington, and Madison Avenue is not only ineffective, it is counterproductive.

"Whose family? Whose values?" The answer to both questions is "God's." Let's begin to live what we believe.